MANNA
In the wilderness of
AIDS

WITHDRAWN
FROM
UNIVERSITY OF PENNSYLVANIA
LIBRARIES

MANNA
In the wilderness of
AIDS

Ten Lessons in Abundance

Kenwyn K. Smith

THE
PILGRIM
PRESS
Cleveland

In honor of
our beloved sisters, brothers,
children, parents, and friends
who died of AIDS

The Pilgrim Press, 700 Prospect Avenue East
Cleveland, Ohio 44115-1100, U.S.A.
pilgrimpress.com

© 2002 Kenwyn K. Smith

All rights reserved. Published 2002

The royalties from this book are being donated to the support of children in Africa living with HIV, many of whom are orphans, having lost both parents to AIDS.

Printed in the United States of America on acid-free paper

Library of Congress Cataloging-in-Publication Data

Smith, Kenwyn K.
    MANNA in the wilderness of AIDS : ten lessons in abundance /
Kenwyn K. Smith.
        p.   cm.
    ISBN 0-8298-1458-2 (alk. paper)
    1. Church work with the sick. 2. AIDS (Disease) – Religious aspects –
Christianity. 3. MANNA (Organization). I. Title.

BV4460.7 .S63 2002
261.8′321969792 – dc21

                                                          2001054880

BREAD FROM HEAVEN
Exodus 16:1–35

The whole community of the Israelites set out from Elim and forty-five days after their departure from Egypt entered the wilderness of Zin, which lies between Elim and Sinai.

The whole congregation of the Israelites complained to Moses and Aaron in the wilderness and said, "It would have been better to die at the Lord's hand back there in Egypt where there was plenty of meat and bread to eat; you brought us out of slavery into this wilderness where we will starve to death!"

The Lord said to Moses, "I will rain down bread from heaven for you. Each day, the people shall go out and gather enough for that day. I will also test them and see whether they will follow my instructions: on the sixth day, when they prepare what they bring in, it will be twice as much as they gathered on other days."

Moses and Aaron said to all the Israelites, "In the evening you shall know that it was the Lord who brought you out of Egypt, and in the morning you will see the glory of the Lord, because he has heard your complaints against him; it is not against us that you bring your complaints; we are nothing. You shall know this," Moses said, "when the Lord, in answer to your complaints, gives you flesh to eat in the evening, and in the morning plenty of bread. For what are we? Your complaints are against the Lord, not us."

Then Moses told Aaron to say to the whole community of Israel, "Draw near to the Lord, for he has heard your complaints." While Aaron was speaking to all the assembled, they looked toward the wilderness and the glory of the Lord appeared in the cloud.

The Lord spoke to Moses and said, "I have heard the complaining of the Israelites. Say to them, 'At twilight you shall eat meat, and in the morning you shall have your fill of bread. Then you shall know that I am the Lord your God.'"

In the evening quails came up and covered the camp. And in the morning there was a layer of dew around the camp. When the layer of dew lifted there on the surface of the wilderness was a fine flaky substance, as fine as frost on the ground.

When the Israelites first saw it they were so amazed they said, "What is it?" for they did not know what it was. Moses said to them, "It is the bread that the Lord has given you to eat.

This is what the Lord has commanded. "Gather as much of it as each of you needs, an omer [a small, but adequate portion] a person according to the number of persons, all providing for those in your own tents."

The Israelites did so, some gathering more, some less. But when they measured it, those who gathered much had nothing over, and those who had gathered little had no shortage. They gathered as much as each of them needed.

And Moses said to them, "Let no one leave any of it over until the morning." But they did not listen to Moses; some left part of it until the next day and it bred worms and became foul. And Moses was angry with them.

Morning by morning they gathered as much as each needed, but when the sun grew hot it melted.

On the sixth day they gathered twice as much food, two omers apiece. When all the leaders of the congregation came and told Moses, he said to them, "This is what the Lord has commanded: 'tomorrow is a day of solemn rest, a holy sabbath to the Lord; bake what you want to bake and boil what you want to boil, and all that is left over put aside to be kept until morning.'"

So they put it aside until morning, as Moses had commanded them; and it did not become foul, and there were no worms in it.

Moses said, "Eat it today, for today is the sabbath to the Lord; today you will not find it in the field. Six days shall you gather it; but on the seventh day, which is a sabbath, there will be none."

On the seventh day some of the people went out to gather, and they found none.

The Lord said to Moses, "How long will you refuse to keep my commandments and instructions? See! The Lord has given you the sabbath; therefore on the sixth day he gives you food for two days; each of you stay where you are; do not leave your place on the seventh day." So the people rested on the seventh day.

The house of Israel called it manna [the Hebrew for "what is it" was *mon hu* — manna in English]. It was like coriander seed, white, and the taste of it was like wafers made with honey. Moses said, "This is what the Lord has commanded: 'Let an omer of it be kept throughout your generations, in order that they may see the food with which I fed you in the wilderness, when I brought you out of the Land of Egypt.'"

And Moses said to Aaron, "Take a jar, and put an omer of manna in it, and place it before the Lord, to be kept throughout the generations." As the Lord commanded Moses, so Aaron placed it before the covenant, for safekeeping.

The Israelites ate manna for forty years, until they came to a habitable land; they ate manna until they came to the border of the land of Canaan.

CONTENTS

ACKNOWLEDGMENTS

I BEGIN BY THANKING MANNA's co-founders (Walla Demp-sey, Mary Gainer, Kay Keenze, Reid Reames, Bob Prischak, and Dixie Scoles) along with the thousands of clients, staff, volunteers, and donors who became the MANNA community.

It is a daunting task to acknowledge all who shaped me during the writing of this book. Some influences were subtle. Others were bold and unmistakable. All were important. With a full heart I acknowledge all the gifts of those who instructed me.

I am grateful to those who read part or all of the manuscript and provided valuable help: Gene Bay, Bill Arnold, Walter Brueggemann, David Berg, Clay Alderfer, Gloria Guard, Mary Ann Phillips, Sara Corse, Greg Goldman, Jamie O'Neill, Dana Kaminstein, Dianne Wilkinson, Joyce François, Judy Rous, and Patricia Burns. I also thank my agent, Mike Hamilburg, and my publisher, Timothy Staveteig, for their assistance.

I especially appreciate the contributions of my Social Work graduate students at the University of Pennsylvania who were members of my fall 1996 class on "Group, Organizational, and Community Dynamics." Their 250 hours of interviews and observations of MANNA, together with copious field notes and commentaries, were a great help.

I thank the University of Pennsylvania for the sabbatical leave that provided me the dedicated time to write this book, Green College, Oxford University, which provided me a scholarly environment in which to work, and the Conkey family, whose garage loft offered me a retreat where no one could find me.

And lastly I thank Sara for being an ever-supportive partner throughout my involvement with MANNA and in the
preparation of this manuscript. For all her love and care and
that of our three children, Phillip, Kalila, and Justin, I am
deeply grateful.

Introduction

MODEST BEGINNINGS

T HIS BOOK IS ABOUT AIDS. My intention is to highlight what we can learn from the most vulnerable in our midst; to demonstrate how the ravines that separate people can be traversed; to document how a vibrant organization can come into being when a few committed individuals take a leap of faith together; to illustrate the abundance that exists in a world of seeming scarcity; and to illuminate how the miraculous resides in the everyday.

This book incorporates several strands of contemporary social thought. I hope to provide a fresh view of volunteerism, especially the kind seeded by communities of faith; to contribute to a growing dialogue between spirituality and social work; to portray a vision of community ministry in a secular age. I want to pour soul into organizational thinking.

This book is for community builders, members of the healing professions, social workers, leaders in our communities of faith, citizens encouraging volunteerism, students of organizational behavior, executives of non-profit organizations, fundraisers, trainees in community ministry, wage-earners contemplating their charitable giving options, managers organizing service opportunities for workers, and individuals thinking about becoming volunteers in the not-for-profit world.

A Time for Rebirth

In the latter half of the 1980s the First Presbyterian Church in downtown Philadelphia was reeling. Our beloved pastor

1

of twenty-five years, Dr. Ernest Sommerville, had died un-expectedly. His invitations to notice the Almighty's presence in every part of our lives, to treat our daily labors as also God's work, to sing praises to Yahweh morning, noon, and night, still reverberated like elongated echoes. However, we were a wounded, grieving community and were feeling keenly God's silence. For many months we were turned inward as we tried to find a healing balm.

The church's reaction to our loss was to keep things as they had always been, not to deviate from the course set by Dr. Sommerville. However, a wise interim pastor suggested we see this as a time for rebirth. This emboldened a small group of us to take an initiative that impacted our lives in ways we could never have anticipated.

For years our church had cooked casseroles for the home-less, run a tutoring program, and given a portion of our resources to agencies providing basic services to the needy.[1] However, some felt it was time for a fresh initiative. The question was what to do.

We considered several possibilities that fit our congre-gation's self-image. But none of these energized us. Then someone said, "Let's ask what our church is most ignoring, for whatever we are working to avoid is probably what we should embrace." To a person we immediately knew what that was. AIDS. All around us people were dying from AIDS, and our church was acting as if this wasn't occurring. Right away we were stirred by the idea of going toward what we were col-lectively avoiding. Before that first meeting was over we had resolved to build a project around AIDS.

Since none of us had a relationship with the AIDS com-munity, we first had to break out of the sociological bubble insulating us. We started by surveying the needs of those with HIV/AIDS and found that in the late 1980s inadequate hous-ing and hunger were the most pressing problems. Building or acquiring homes was beyond us, but food was not. Our project was allocated $4,000 by the church, and we were off and running. Each Monday evening we prepared casseroles and took them to some of our neighbors living with AIDS. At the time we knew nothing about the special nutritional needs of those struggling with the AIDS wasting syndrome. Hence the food we prepared probably provided minimal nourishment for the body, but it did get us started and put us on a steep learning curve.

Initially the church accepted our AIDS project, but that was soon to change. The demand for our meals was overwhelming, and when we decided to mount a larger effort some opposition within the congregation emerged. Our $4,000 budget was meager, and the church coffers would soon be empty if we did but a fraction of what was needed. A few insiders using the kitchen once a week had posed no threat, but, as one sweet eighty-year-old expressed it, "People with AIDS will be coming in and spreading all kinds of diseases to innocent people." In the 1980s the general public still knew little about HIV/AIDS, and our congregation was no exception. Such reactions had to be confronted. Delicately.

No Turning Back

During those first months we learned how much people living with AIDS felt shunned by the community. Some said they thought they were being treated like modern-day lepers. We understood why they felt this way. The face of AIDS was tough to look at and had evoked in us emotions we wanted to avoid. Many were economically devastated and were so sick it was a struggle for them to maintain the basics. Bodies were emaciated, mental health was precarious, and spirits were crushed. Immediately we recognized the food we brought was important, but what it symbolized was even more critical. It wasn't just bread for the day. It was an affirmation that the community still cared.

Something happened to our collective spirits that first year, and as the demand for our meals grew, we knew there was no turning back. We were learning so much about our society, ourselves, our community of faith. For the next year we continued with our Monday night cooking and delivery of meals to the few we could serve and also worked vigorously to form a non-profit, volunteer-based, organization. That protected our church from legal and financial risks, let people from all walks of life join us, and in time rekindled the congregation's support.

In January 1990, our new organization was established. We elected to call it MANNA, an acronym for Metropolitan AIDS Neighborhood Nutrition Alliance. The choice of a name had a strong impact on our unfolding history. As we brainstormed about names, biblical terms like "Our Daily Bread" and "manna" kept recurring. None of us were imbued with an unusual faith. We all felt more attuned to our doubts and our uncertainties than to our faith. This was why the term "MANNA" was appealing. We felt an identification with the Jews wandering through the wilderness in search of the Promised Land.

As we engaged in the planning it was self-evident that we had much to learn, both about HIV and the role of nutrition in the lives of those with AIDS, that we had no idea where to get the resources needed to build and operate this organization, that it would require significant faith, not only our own but that of anyone willing to support us, and that despite the fact that logic said we could not possibly succeed we should proceed anyway. To ignore AIDS and those suffering at the hands of this deadly virus was to turn our back on the calling of both humanitarianism and our faith.

Our mission was clear and straightforward: to ensure that in the Philadelphia region, no man, woman, or child who was homebound and ill with HIV/AIDS ever went hungry again. We also had a deeper purpose. While we hoped the meals would help sustain withering bodies, our primary goal was to walk daily into the lives of those with HIV/AIDS, many of whom had been abandoned by family, friends, and the society, and to express, on behalf of the community as a whole, the love and care we would all want if any of us were in similar circumstances. The physical food was the gift, but the repeated assurance that the community still cared was the real message. And, like the sweet bread offered to those in the ancient desert, MANNA's meals would be free.

Key Principles

We decided to operate MANNA as a volunteer organization, with the job of paid staff being to support the labor of the volunteers. All tasks would be packaged in "bite-sized chunks" so no one would be overburdened; the cumulative effect of many small actions would have a potent effect. Further, we would view MANNA as an agent of the larger community of which we were a part.

We constructed four pictures of how MANNA would operate. Any persons seeking MANNA's services had only to call, give us their address, and provide some information about dietary restrictions based on their medical condition. Within twenty-four hours MANNA would start delivering meals. The clients had to agree to be home at noon or to give us an alternative drop-off arrangement if they had a doctor's appointment or some other commitment. It was pointed out that this service was for those with AIDS who were too ill to care for themselves. If this described their condition, no further questions would be asked.

Once the call was received we planned to computerize the relevant information and assign volunteers to make deliveries Monday through Friday. The food would be prepared by volunteers under the supervision of a qualified chef whose primary role would be to create the menu, purchase the food, and ensure that the proper nutrition was offered, given each individual's medical and dietary conditions.

For the volunteers there would be three kinds of work. They could serve on a kitchen crew three to four hours once a week, deliver meals one lunchtime a week, or help with administrative duties such as staffing phones and sending out mail.

In the community MANNA hoped to build links with other AIDS agencies, such as the medical clinics and those doing case management. Clients with no case manager or doctor would be connected with appropriate help. We were clear that our goal was to complement what was currently being done and not to replicate or compete with any existing services.

We developed a business plan, laid out the staff required as we went from delivering twenty, to fifty, then a hundred meals, spelled out the facilities and equipment needed (kitchen, office space, van, phones, computers, walk-in freezers), strategized about how to get good produce at low cost, searched for the nutritional advice we needed, and produced a funding plan.

Then we ran into a roadblock. The task of writing multiple proposals and making scores of overtures to institutions asking for resources was so labor intensive it seemed impossible. Also the dollars available for AIDS work in Philadelphia at that time were so limited that the established organizations did not need another agency making claims on the same pot of resources. We felt we should not go to the same wells other AIDS agencies relied upon. That meant MANNA had to invent or dig up new funding streams. No matter how we looked at it the task seemed impossible. In spite of this we went ahead and the seven of us who began this organization and were later referred to as the "founders" became the board of directors, cooks, clean-up crew, managers, meal deliverers, and fund-raisers.

We were soon to learn that most of those receiving

MANNA's meals were in the last months of their lives. Since the prejudices against people with AIDS in the 1980s were severe, individuals kept their medical status secret until it could no longer be hidden. That usually occurred when the wasting syndrome kicked in, which was almost impossible to reverse once severe weight loss occurred. MANNA was to become a ministry to the dying, and we were called upon to be among the grievers each time one of the larger MANNA family died.

By the end of 1996 all seven "founders" had stepped aside from our formal roles in MANNA. At that time a thousand meals were being delivered six days a week to people living with HIV/AIDS in the greater Philadelphia area. Some 650 volunteers were working weekly under the guidance of eleven full-time staff, making MANNA a truly vibrant organization. The annual operating budget was $1 million and more than three thousand people were contributing to MANNA's finances. MANNA had moved out of the church into a row house restaurant and was preparing to move into a permanent home, one where it would be possible to prepare twenty-five hundred meals a day. This facility was being reconstructed, and a capital campaign of $1 million had been launched. Over six thousand individuals had received MANNA meals, and we had collectively grieved the death of hundreds of our brothers, sisters, and children.

In Retrospect

This book describes several critical lessons we learned during the early years of MANNA's life. I was chair of MANNA's board of directors for its first six and a half years and want to document my view of MANNA's inception, infancy, and childhood. I am grateful to Walla Dempsey, Mary Gainer, Dixie Scoles, Kay Keenze, Reid Reames, and Bob Prischak, with whom and from whom I learned so much. Not a single insight recorded in this book would have been possible had it not been for the journey we seven took together. However, as the recorder of this shared story I take responsibility for how my experiences, leadership, and interpretations of events shaped this narrative. I know that the other six members of our group would highlight different features of the journey and that the light that shone so bright would be refracted through a different facet of the prism, but we would each be speaking about the same light. Hundreds and hundreds of people worked to bring MANNA to life. Many gave their souls to this organization, its mission, and its day-to-day chores. Along with the people we served, they were the real authors of this story. I salute them all.

When we began we thought we were responding to the universal command to "do unto others as you would have them do unto you," and the specific instruction of our faith to feed the hungry, clothe the naked, embrace the downtrodden. We viewed this as a ministry to others. How surprised we were to find that walking hand-in-hand with those passing through the valley of the shadow of death opened our hearts to important lessons for our own lives. Today I see MANNA's early years as a contemporary version of that ancient account of Moses and the Israelites as we trekked through the modern-day wilderness of AIDS. What MANNA learned was so rich and provocative, I want its story in the public domain. I am eager for students in many disciplines and people from all walks of life to consider these lessons, especially those working to create and sustain community and volunteer-based organizations.

I have struggled long and hard about how to craft this narrative. There were several dimensions to my equivocations.

I am an organizational psychologist, working as an academic at the University of Pennsylvania and consulting to organizations embroiled in conflict. I teach human development and group, organizational, and community dynamics to graduate students at the University of Pennsylvania's School of Social Work and the Fels Institute of Government. I also spend long hours in the classroom with international executives at the Wharton Business School as we wrestle with topics like managing conflict, organizational change, and leadership. At MANNA I was able to apply the leadership theories, group relations principles, and managerial practices that I have studied and taught for years.

Through this book the reader can see what worked and what didn't. I was delighted when I saw the concepts from my field having a powerful and positive impact on MANNA's functioning. I was disturbed when, despite our best intentions, we made mistakes that we knew we should avoid. Overall, however, I am proud of what we achieved together.

I have worked hard to represent the truths as we lived them at the time, neither diminishing nor enlarging reality. Where possible I use the voices of those whose experiences are reported. I draw mostly upon the stories told to members of a graduate class at Penn who studied MANNA for a semester in the mid-1990s and thousands of pages of field notes and file entries that constituted my record from the period I was chair of the board.[2] I must say that had I not lived the MANNA experience myself I probably would not have believed some of what is found in these pages. I have done what I can to describe our shared realities, occasionally taking a little literary license and on a couple of occasions even "fictionalizing" a context to protect the identities of those whose privacy must be preserved. In order to be consistent all names are pseudonyms, even those whose actions were so public their identities will be recognized by people who know this organization well. I have done my best to represent the truth contained within the MANNA story.

One thing was difficult for me as author. The human side of this enterprise was only a part of the story. There was also a transcendent quality to much of what happened, even as we stirred the stew, got upset when a meal deliverer's car became stuck in a snow bank, or fretted about where the money would come from to pay that month's bills. I will discuss the spirit active at MANNA, although we did not have a common vocabulary for talking about this aspect of our organization. By 1996 the MANNA community had several thousand members, including donors, clients, and volunteers, and was made up of a generous mixture of Christians, atheists, Taoists, Jews, humanists, Hindus, Buddhists, Muslims, nihilists, agnostics. An assortment of philosophies one might use to guide one's actions existed in our midst. What we learned together existed in the human domain, but it had a spiritual dimension, whether one called it God, Tau, Yahweh, a Higher Power, the Almighty, Oneness, Buddha, or the Great Spirit. While we lacked a common language to talk about the spirit in our midst, no one missed the fact that we were a highly spirited bunch. I wish there were an easy and inclusive way to talk about this part of MANNA that faithfully captured the interpretations of all. However, there isn't, so I have chosen to use the spiritual motif that makes most sense to me, the original manna story as experienced by the Israelites of old escaping slavery in Egypt. God's gifts of "bread from heaven" are at the heart of Jewish, Muslim, and Christian thought, and similar constructions exist in many spiritual traditions.

Major Lessons

This reflection highlights the most significant things learned during the infancy and development of MANNA, the first seven years (1990–96). Each chapter is dedicated to an essential lesson.

1. Whenever we were lost someone appeared to show us the way.

2. The greatest insights came from the most vulnerable in our midst.

3. The "leaps of faith" we took filled our spirits with vitality.

4. MANNA's vulnerabilities were its strengths, and its strengths were its vulnerabilities.

5. Love grew when given away.

6. MANNA became an importer of pain; it had to learn how to manage pain internally and not become an exporter of blame.

7. MANNA changed how we looked at the world.

8. To thrive in the midst of massive turbulence demanded deep roots and radical shifts carefully timed.

9. MANNA both sharpened and healed the tensions of race and social class.

10. The miraculous was contained within the mundane.

My files are filled with stories that bear testimony to the impact AIDS and MANNA had on our lives. I am anguished about all those I did not include, folks who gave so much to make MANNA possible, clients who touched so many hearts, volunteers and donors whose generosity knew no bounds. I had to select but a fragment from the whole array of experiences; otherwise this book would become several volumes. My selections were driven by my wish to offer both a representation of the whole and to highlight what I felt was most important. As the AIDS scene changes it would be easy to let our beginnings fade in importance. The manna story, which belongs to both the ages and the present, must never be forgotten!

One

LOST AND LIBERATED

Lesson 1:
Whenever we were lost someone appeared
to show us the way.

W HEN SARA AND I discovered she was carrying twins I
excitedly called a buddy of mine and blurted out, "My
wife's having two babies. I can hardly imagine coping with
one! I need a course on fathering twins." A recent dad himself,
he said, "Let your kids be your teacher. They'll know the kind
of father they need. Be open to learning from them." MANNA
started with a similar spirit. We decided to let those we served
be our instructors, to just start cooking and delivering meals
and see what we learned.

Nora

Our first teacher was Nora, a fifty-year-old African American grandmother who quickly took us under her wing. Both
she and her former husband had been struggling with HIV
for years. For the last year of her life, we visited her in pairs,
a couple of times a week, bringing bags of groceries and a
hot meal. No matter how ill she was, Nora insisted we stay
and chat with her. She'd tell us in detail how she was feeling,
what it took to digest the foods we had brought on our previous visit, how her last trip to the hospital had been. This
helped us see the unpredictability of AIDS, the almost daily
fluctuations she had to live with, that she had both good days

and bad. When Nora was well she was joyful, but when ill she surrendered to whatever the virus deemed for that day.

Nora would ask probing questions about how we filled our days, what sparked our passions, what gave our life meaning. She spoke with pride about her son serving in the military, excitedly described the research her daughter was doing for her Ph.D., shared with us the struggles of her fifteen-year-old who was terrified of being without a mother. Often one of her adult children would drop by while we were there. She particularly loved it when her grandson was present. She insisted we keep a distance from her if she was throwing up, unless we had protective gloves on. Nora also made it clear that she fed her children and grandson from the food we brought before she would ever eat anything herself.

Each visit, no matter how sick she felt, Nora chose to tell us something special about her own story. Initially we wondered why she did this. Was she just making conversation? Did she need to say out loud what her life had been like? Was she attempting to convey a message to us? In time we came to understand what she was trying to communicate to us: here we were taking food to a dying lady who lived in a cockroach-infested apartment rented from the City Housing Authority; being with her regularly left us feeling anxious, helpless, and upset; yet when we returned to our own homes we always felt emotionally nourished by our time with her.

This dying woman drew us into her heart, and we looked forward to being with her. No week felt right unless we'd spent a little time with Nora. The more we gave of ourselves to her the more we felt loved by her. Each week she reminded us how much she and her family appreciated us. If one of us were unable to be there, she would phone us to check that we were all right. She was as concerned about our well-being as we were about hers.

Nora was clear that the only relationship she wanted was one that felt reciprocal. She was willing to receive from us so long as we were open to receiving from her. The mutuality had to be real. During those months Nora showed us how critical it was to let the meal recipient decide what kind of relationship she or he wanted to have with MANNA's volunteers and taught us to accept whatever form of connectedness the client wished.

It is a decade since Nora died, but I still can still picture her face, recall the sound of her voice, imagine what she would say about something distressing me, and feel her presence. No week goes by without some little event reminding me of her.

MANNA volunteers tell story after story that makes it clear that the HIV world is filled with people like Nora. To begin with I was surprised that there was so much nourishment available to us within the ranks of the needy. Now I understand it differently. The very act of receiving a simple gift like MANNA's food, prepared with caring hands and offered with loving hearts, releases the "Nora-like spirit" dormant in both the receiver and the giver.

"God's Love"

While we were planning to form MANNA, our group went to visit a meals program in New York City called "God's Love We Deliver." We were eager to learn from their experiences. When we arrived it was suggested the best way to take it in would be to put on an apron and work. We willingly undertook the tasks assigned us, had a great time, and left New York feeling uplifted by the spirit that had infused our day. That visit helped us see what was possible and was a rich catalyst.

The key message we received that day was "just do it." We were counseled to do our planning, but not to tarry. The message was this: "There are people out there dying of starvation and they need food today; choose a date and get going; people will call; helpers will show up; the resources you need will come in."

The question was how to begin. We could not wait until we had built the elaborate infrastructure we would eventually need. There were too many people in Philadelphia ill with AIDS and in desperate need of food. Saying "sorry, we are not ready" was not an option. There was also the question of how to fold into MANNA the people we had been serving over the previous year and a half.

Borrowing from "God's Love," we decided to begin as follows. Upon receiving a call asking for MANNA's help, we would approach a restaurant and ask it to donate a hot meal at noon each weekday. We would then locate volunteers who lived or worked near this restaurant and ask them to pick up the meal and deliver it to the recipient's home. In those early days everyone who called MANNA had an established residence. It was quite some time before we confronted how to deliver to the homeless with AIDS.

We put a new phone line in one of our homes, called the major AIDS agencies and medical clinics serving people with HIV, told them MANNA was in business, and awaited the first call. Within a few hours, the phone rang. The call was from Ben, a thirty-five-year-old man who had only in recent weeks told his parents that he was gay and that he was dying from AIDS. He was to be the recipient of MANNA's first meal. It was late Thursday afternoon, so we took his particulars and told him that meal deliveries would begin the next Monday and would continue each weekday for as long as he needed.

Having made this commitment, the task was to find a restaurant willing to donate meals to Ben every noon and a group of volunteers who would deliver the food to him, Monday through Friday. The reality was simple. We would find the needed help or do the cooking and make the deliveries ourselves. This was how the member of our group who took on the task of organizing meals for Ben described the experience: "I set to work and spent the afternoon riding a bicycle around Philadelphia looking for a restaurant owner willing to give Ben a meal five days a week. I visited eighteen restaurants but couldn't find a single owner. Many of the employees I met said they were sure their boss would help, but no one was in the position to commit resources.

"As I pensively rode my bike back to work wondering what to do next I mindlessly passed the building that housed the cafeteria for employees at my organization. A block later my inner voice said, 'Wake up, man! Why didn't you think of the employee cafeteria?' I turned my bike around, went in, and found the manager, whom I had never met before, and asked if he could help. Within two minutes he had agreed to donate a three-course meal every workday at noon.

"The next task was to find volunteers to deliver the meals to Ben. I quickly mobilized a group of my friends and was moved by how many were willing to help. However, before I had even got them organized the answer machine was buzzing with news of a second person seeking MANNA's services. I rang the cafeteria manager and asked if he could increase the number of meals to two. Without hesitation he said 'Yes.' On my fifth call to him he laughed and said, 'There's no need to keep calling. Just assume I'll agree to whatever you request.' Within a short time we were picking up ten delicious three-course meals every noon prepared by the chefs in his kitchen."

With each new person asking for MANNA's meals an additional group of delivery volunteers had to be found. Eager to avoid overcommitment and burnout, we were determined to limit the tasks we asked of volunteers. Most said they could easily deliver once a week. Hence each new person in need of meals required the creation of a group of five new volunteers.

It was fascinating to see where MANNA's volunteers came from and how people responded to our requests. For example, this was the experience of one of our group the first day she started recruiting helpers for MANNA:

"I was meeting with a senior executive in another department at my office. We were engrossed in a conversation about a complex problem when this executive suddenly looked at his watch and said, 'I'm sorry; we'll have to continue some other time. I'm already late for my weekly staff meeting.' Seizing the initiative, I asked, 'Would you mind if I come to your staff meeting for a few minutes to discuss an issue unrelated to work?' I knew this man fairly well, but was surprised when he said, 'Sure,' without even asking me what I wanted to do.

"Once we got to his staff meeting I went directly to the point. I introduced them to MANNA and told them that I needed a group of volunteers to start delivering meals to someone who called just that morning. 'When would we start?' a man asked. 'Tomorrow,' I replied. 'How long are we to do it?' 'In this case, for the rest of his life.' Within three minutes six of them took on the task. I thanked them, and left."

That group faithfully made the deliveries to Charlie every weekday until he died five months later.

The first few weeks were a whirlwind for our group of seven as we tried to get MANNA started. Several of us spent every free moment asking restaurants for food and hustling our friends, colleagues, and acquaintances into becoming MANNA meal deliverers. We were overwhelmed by the number of requests we received but were equally astonished by how many people were willing to help. Within a few weeks the MANNA family consisted of thirty meal recipients, scores of volunteers, and close to twenty Philadelphia restaurants.

During these first few months we also started planning to open our own kitchen. Organizing restaurant meals was extremely labor intensive and with increasing numbers, we had to think about how to best use our energies. We were also learning about the nutritional requirements of those suffering from the AIDS wasting syndrome and realized that meals had to be tailored to match the fluctuations and changes in our clients' dietary needs. Getting our own chef and doing our own cooking was our next task.

One day the member of our group who organized the meals that came from his workplace cafeteria dropped by to thank the manager for his contributions. This was how he described what transpired:

"I walked in feeling guilty for not having thanked them earlier. This manager and his chefs were so very generous, and I had not even extended them the courtesy of a formal thank-you. As I started to speak, the manager interrupted me.

" 'You've come in here to thank me! Don't you dare!' he said.

"The force with which he stopped my thank-you startled me. I wondered if I should be more apologetic about my tardiness, but his next statement took my anxiety away. 'You've got it all wrong. I should be thanking you!'

" 'Why?' I asked.

" 'Because you have solved my morale problem. For months my chefs and kitchen staff have been in the doldrums. I have tried every managerial technique I know to turn around the climate in this place, all to no avail. However, preparing meals for MANNA did it within days. Suddenly they have a purpose they can all relate to, they come in happy in the morning, they now sort out their problems among themselves, and when they need help from me they ask for it. All this began to change when I invited them to prepare meals for people living with AIDS. Once they started putting their heart into one part of their work the positive affect began to spread into their other responsibilities, all because we asked them to give something of themselves instead of offering to pay them more for their labor. This has taught me more about the art of management than any course I've taken and my many years of experience. Thank you. Thank you. Thank you.' "

As we listened to this account, we were in awe of the wellsprings MANNA was beginning to tap.

The Wealth of Volunteers

From the beginning we were overwhelmed and delighted by the volunteers who came to work with us. They brought us their energy, their labor, and their adventurousness and were never reluctant to share what they were learning. After working for a couple of years Jeff and Fran wrote the following account of their experiences.

"We started delivering almost by accident. I had recently retired, and we were looking for something nice to do that would give something back. Fran was in a dance class with one of MANNA's founders. The coincidence sent us a message, and after debating awhile we stepped on board.

"For us the personal effect has been deep and fulfilling, an enriched understanding of self, awakening to a different world. One could not see and meet the world of Philadelphia without being aroused from the sleep of the middle class. The quiet courage of those afflicted and of those who stand by them is inspirational.

"We've occasionally headed home after a day's volunteering sad and drained, but always enriched, always glad we made the hour-and-a-half, round-trip journey. The early days were the toughest. Many lovely people departed. Neither of us had really dealt with death.

"If we have any rule, it is that we shake hands, touch each client. The media has created a public perception of AIDS as the modern-day leprosy, its victims as pariahs. They are not. They are decent, caring people, friends to us. We let the client determine the amount of interaction. Some want anyone to talk to immediately. Some who are initially shy, on finding a friendly presence, gradually open up, while a few avoid interaction, period.

"We feel we're working from the corner we're in. We can't change the world; we can affect those we touch personally. These few vignettes are exemplary of the myriad marvelous snippets of life we've seen and lived; a rich panoply seeming much deeper and more intense than the limited time period of our involvement.

"Jim, a long-term client, one of the finest persons we've met, became gradually more ill. The closest to a complaint we ever heard from him was when, with his weight at maybe seventy pounds, he said 'I'm not a happy camper.' Shortly thereafter, he was transferred into a barren environment in a nursing home. We visited Jim in the home and learned of the possibility of transfer to Calcutta House, a hospice founded by Mother Teresa. Jim knew time was short. He wanted and needed a world of love and feeling. The result was remarkable! He was transferred to Calcutta House, and Jim became a happy camper. We visited him there and got to know the nuns — incredible people.

"On what turned out to be our last visit, Jim held Fran's hand the whole time, a first. Finally leaving, we turned for some reason at the end of the long hallway and looked back. Jim, who could not lift his head, had somehow risen up in the bed and was waving goodbye. Back in the car, we compared impressions and felt Jim was offering his final farewell. Several days later we visited again. Jim had died that morning.

"Saundra, Darren, and Karen, a mother, father, and two-year-old daughter we've been delivering to, is our fourth family contact. Both parents are HIV positive, and we just hope for their daughter, as they do. This experience again illustrates the infinite variety of victims of AIDS — in direct contradiction to the disturbingly monochromatic, puritanical picture painted by the media, echoed by mainstream society.

"Quiet courage in the face of sad acts of fate and injustice are the norm. Sonny, a present client, is a forty-one-year-old father of nine, with staples in his stomach from shrapnel in Vietnam. He receives $11 a month in food stamps; to collect them he must negotiate a four-mile round-trip — despite the fact that in the last six weeks he has suffered pneumonia, a series of strokes, a suspected brain tumor, a brain biopsy, and hospitalization four times. Last Tuesday Sonny was evicted, thrown into the street, by his slumlord's thugs, in the midst of a snowstorm, for being two weeks late in his rent. Still, no complaint.

"Lew never complained. A stevedore, he discovered on one horrible day when his foot was crushed by a two-ton chimney that he was HIV positive. When we expressed shock and sadness, he said he felt very lucky. Why? I have forgotten.

"Postscript: Lew died a hero yesterday a week after we last saw him. His house had collapsed and, to quote the *Inquirer*, 'Just as the floor gave way, two strong arms reached out to Cora Wright and engulfed her in a protective embrace. "Don't let go. We're going to be all right." Lew saved my life,' said Cora in tears when she found that he had given his own.

"Lew was our first delivery and longest relationship, well over two years. In early December of last year, Fran suggested we should visit Lew's mother, Jean, that day and drop off some things (a watercolor I'd done of Lew, a house plant with special meaning for Jean, and some Christmas gifts). As we pulled up for the first time in months, Jean ran out, hugged us and said 'I knew you'd be here!' It turned out it was the first anniversary of Lew's death. We had a joyous reunion with Jean and Lew's sister and brother, who had taken the day off from work because Jean had told them we would definitely be there. Fran had remembered only the general time frame of Lew's demise. We concluded that, in some strange way, it must be a wonderful world! This is a family labeled 'severely dysfunctional.' Most families I've seen should be this together, caring, and functional.

"The rewards for us personally are exemplified in some way by an experience not involving clients directly at all. We were delivering to an even more destitute neighborhood than usual when Fran heard the sound of a kitten crying from an abandoned house on the corner. A large man, Fred, was standing in the boarded-up doorway of the house. On the sidewalk an elderly street person, Ronnie, warmed by a fire in an oil drum, was working on metal junk parts.

"Fran, who loves all creatures, inquired if the kitten might be rescued. Eventually she and Fred climbed through an open window to investigate. Trapped high inside the walls they found two tiny starving kittens.

"Tim, the client we were delivering to, arrived on the scene and said he had been wanting a kitten and would take both of them. Since he had little money to spare, we decided to get some kitten food. As we headed over to the store, Ronnie, the unfriendly looking street person, called over to us and asked if we were going to the store. Having noticed the several pairs of ragged gloves on his hands, the three crusty hats on his toothless head, we braced ourselves for a request for money or food. 'This is for the kittens,' he said. He handed Fran a ratty, wrinkled dollar bill.

"But what to do? Such compassion, kindness, and humanity in the midst of terrible poverty deserved something. We decided to try friendship. We had found that Ronnie sold the torn-up metals to junkyards. That week we started setting aside worn-out appliances, cans, things made of aluminum, steel, brass. We gradually expanded to clothing and canned foods. Acquaintances grew as we dropped our collections off. We found that Fred, employed at Vets Stadium, is like Ronnie's guardian in the neighborhood. We began to notice subtle changes in Ronnie. He started looking younger; his previously inane babble became gradually intelligible. Finally, I gave him a copy of my last book. He, to our surprise, wound up reading every word and quizzed me relentlessly on things I'd almost forgotten I wrote. Once, after we'd almost failed to recognize him with his improving appearance, we discovered from Fred that Ronnie was not in his sixties; he was in his early forties with a son in college in New Jersey.

"Now, three years later, Ronnie has gone back to school. He has completed one year in a city-sponsored job training program that he attends four days a week. His son has started visiting him, and his outward persona has continued to improve. Don't get us wrong. Ronnie is still Ronnie — a totally natural, generous (he has tried to force money on me many times) person who is not likely to ever fit into our society's world of work, even though he works harder than I ever did. But he looks odd and is completely open and honest. A rough combination in this society.

"Our larger families have become involved, saving aluminum cans, clothes, an assortment of other things for Ronnie to use. Ronnie's neighbors have grown accustomed to seeing us visit the area to drop things off and now shout greetings and stop to chat.

"To see a being bloom and a neighborhood gather in support is remarkable. The overall experience is indescribable. Words pale. This adventure, mostly unrelated to delivering meals, epitomizes MANNA for us."

Postscript: several years later Fran reported that, "due to a degenerative disease, my husband, Jeff, has become wheelchair bound and has lost all speech, although his brain is still very active and delightedly he can still write and make good use of his laptop. I often think of our days volunteering at MANNA. You know, one person who still calls us regularly to ask how Jeff is doing and to offer him words of encouragement is Lew's mother, Jean. We are so grateful for the special friendships we made through MANNA."

"I Can Work Full Time — For Free"

Within months of MANNA's beginning we were desperate for full-time staff. We had appointed our first executive director, and we were about to open our own kitchen, hire a chef, and do our own cooking. The pressing need was for someone to run the daily operations: receive phone calls from those seeking MANNA meals; establish regular contact with each person's physician or case worker; determine the nutritional needs of each client; recruit, train, and manage the volunteers; create kitchen crews to prepare the meals; and organize the distribution of the food to the various neighborhoods. We were trying desperately to invent ways to get funds for this position but had not yet succeeded. We knew we could not go far without such a new hire.

Then one of our inner circle learned that an aunt who had recently died had unexpectedly left her some money. She excitedly informed us she was prepared to leave her job as a corporate executive and take on the task of setting up MANNA's operations. She thought there was enough in her aunt's bequest to let her work for MANNA for almost a year without needing a salary. This occurred right at a point when we were at a loss about what to do. Where were we going to find a bright, vivacious, compassionate, competent senior executive with a first-rate MBA to work in such a job for no pay? Within a few months MANNA had three full-time staff members and a growing, vibrant cadre of volunteers.

The challenge that was most daunting was fund-raising. We started by writing numerous grant applications, but that was too focused on the long term. The review process for foundation funding took months, and MANNA was like an infant in an incubator who might not make it out of babyhood. Our need was for cash to buy the food today, to meet payroll now. Yet we believed that if we never put in place a long-term funding plan we would forever be financially precarious. Little did we realize that for years to come MANNA would be a hand-to-mouth organization, no matter how creative we were in getting money or how many successful grant proposals we wrote.

In the midst of our uncertainty about how to find money and before we had even mapped out the size of the task ahead, a man showed up on our doorstep unannounced. For years this individual had dedicated most of his spare time to raising money for non-profit organizations and recently had devoted all his energies to the well-being of those living with HIV/AIDS. He had lost many friends to AIDS and had used his service to others as a way to express his grief. Within weeks he was functioning as our full-time volunteer fund-raiser. We often worried that his own business might founder while he labored to keep MANNA afloat, but whenever we raised this question with him he dismissed our worries and worked even harder for MANNA.

For almost three years he functioned as a full-time development director. He organized our first annual giving campaign, our first quarterly newsletter, our first almost everything, and drew a host of concerned supporters into the MANNA fold. The talent he recruited was phenomenal. For example, he mobilized highly skilled event organizers and committees consisting of scores of people to run our annual auction called "A Show of Hands." The artists and art donors were of a caliber few of us imagined we'd ever meet, let alone have as friends of MANNA. He also mobilized a large group of fund-raising volunteers to take on many of the tasks critical for MANNA to be stabilized financially. What others could not do, he did himself. Never once did he receive a cent from MANNA for his labors. Even when we thanked him, he insisted that doing the work was reward enough.

Another individual in this early era came close to being a full-time MANNA worker without ever going on the payroll. A few years earlier Julia had closed a restaurant that she had owned and run for more than a decade. When she started volunteering in our kitchen, Julia soon became our chef's assistant, his culinary confidant, his backup. For a couple of years Julia was always at MANNA, up to her elbows in dough, stirring a pot of stew, or taking something delectable from the oven. When we outgrew the capacity of the church, Julia and her husband rented MANNA their former restaurant at a price that we could afford.

During the first few years we also had many architectural needs: organizing walk-in freezers, buying industrial standard stoves, venting the church to meet licensing standards, outfitting the kitchen at Julia's restaurant, organizing work space at first for thirty volunteers, then a hundred, then two hundred, and so forth. As soon as we put anything in place we had to change it. The demand for MANNA's meals grew so fast nothing was stable for more than a few weeks. To make efficient use of our volunteer labor pool our physical space had to be constantly reorganized. Then, when we decided in 1996 to move to a permanent home and begin a capital campaign so MANNA could settle in for the next decade, someone had to transform a rubble-filled expanse into a state-of-the-art facility. Fortunately one of our original group of seven was an architect, and he did all our design work. I took it all for granted at the time, but as I look back I marvel at how much he did to make it possible for MANNA to function. Often he had dealt with our needs before the rest of us realized some more human energy or resources had to be mobilized. He was our rock of Gibraltar. Then when we needed a board secretary or a chair of the long-range planning committee, he quietly took on such tasks as well.

Before today I never added up the dollar value of the labor donated by these four individuals (our operations manager, our assistant chef, our fund-raiser, and our architect) over our first few years. Had we paid professional rates for their services, it would have had to be well over half a million dollars.

The Israelites in the Desert

The founder of "God's Love We Deliver" was right. "When it's God's Love you're dealing with, there is no limit to the

supply." Our clients needed so much just to stay alive. Likewise MANNA needed so much just to get off the ground. Yet
everything we truly required seemed available to us when we
needed it. Over the years the widest range of people appeared
in our lives to educate us, inspire us, sustain us, and show us
the way, especially when we were lost.

At the beginning AIDS was an unfamiliar wilderness to us;
we were a people with no guidebook for the territory in front
of us. That was probably why we felt so drawn to the original
manna story, which of course took place in a real wilderness, a stretch of arid land sandwiched between the Nile and
the Sinai. However, in sacred literatures "the wilderness" was
often used as a metaphor for being in exile or deprived of
all things familiar, an all too common condition for the children of Israel. From the rock where Abraham raised his knife
to sacrifice his beloved son Isaac, through to the waters of
Babylon, these nomads were always at risk as they traveled
across territory that was unfamiliar, both literally and spiritually. When MANNA began those with AIDS clearly felt like
an exiled community, and the unknown territory of AIDS felt
like a wilderness to us.

Today, those heading for the wilderness, be it the outback,
the moon, or the urban jungle, are schooled in the special
skills required to stay alive in hazardous environments. They
are taught what to pack to ensure survival. The Israelites,
however, did not have any prior education. Their learning
was done in the desert. They had set off from Egypt believing
the journey to the promised land would be easy once they
were free of Pharaoh's clutches. That was pure fantasy. After
forty-five days liberated Israel was lost, geographically and
spiritually, although they did not know just how far they had
gone astray. There was no road map for this journey. Where
was this promised land located? And would they have the capacity to recognize it once they arrived? It was to take forty
years to reach their destination. That was a lot of lostness.

The little community that started MANNA was also lost and remained so for a long time. How often we said things like "I am at a complete loss about how to deal with...." We were also spiritually lost. After all, it had been the intensity of our inner barrenness that launched us into the wilderness of AIDS in the first place, in search of a new way to be in the world. When we began we knew nothing about the nutritional requirements of those living with HIV. We had no idea about the kind of caretaking that would be of value to people living with AIDS. And we had no clue about how to get the resources that would be required.

The lesson that the original manna story conveyed, and that MANNA was to relearn, was that whenever we were lost that was only half the story. We might not know where we were, but the Almighty did. God had a keen appreciation of our whereabouts, even when we were without a compass. That was our liberation. Being lost was our first step out of the intellectual boxes that held us captive. I shudder when I think that we might have never experienced our spirits freed had we not been as lost as we were.

There is a beautiful image that has long comforted the indigenous peoples of North America. When lost in the woods and afraid, all I have to do is to stand still and listen to the tranquility all around me. Since the trees, the birds, and all the creatures are not lost, I can be calmed by the assurance that they know where they are. If I stand still and give over to the rhythms of nature the forest will find me. Since nature knows where it is, by fully joining with it I cease to be lost also.

What a compelling concept! When feeling lost, stand still, for the jungle around me is not lost. It knows itself and understands where I am. If I am patient and peacefully listen to the world around me, this powerful stranger will make itself known to me. And as it gets to know me, an outsider, I too will know where and who I am.[3]

The poetic reality is that only those who are lost can be

found, only the confused are positioned to move to a new level of understanding, only the limited are open to noticing the potential located within the constraints. Manna was the assurance to the ancients that they were not lost to the Almighty, that they belonged to the ranks of the beloved. MANNA was also to learn that all who suffered so much at the hands of AIDS and those who witnessed their pain were held close by the heart of God.

Two

DANCING WITH CHILDREN

Lesson 2:
*The greatest insights came
from the most vulnerable in our midst.*

F ROM THE BEGINNING MANNA confronted many issues
that stirred our anxieties, questions like how to connect with people who were different from us, how to preserve
everyone's safety when going into dangerous neighborhoods,
and how to generate the resources needed without distracting
ourselves from our primary mission. Not many organizational
or managerial texts addressed topics like this, at least not in
a form we could readily translate into the AIDS setting. We
soon realized that MANNA was going to have to invent its
own responses to such issues. However, we got great help from
the most unlikely of places.

We were to discover that the most vulnerable in our midst
had many gifts for us that proved to be of lasting value. This
was powerfully illustrated during our early attempts to connect
with Latino families with AIDS, by a special event called "Kids
Care," which gave voice to the artistic passions of children,
and by the annual fund-raiser started by the dancers of the
Pennsylvania Ballet as they struggled to prevent the death of
dance in Philadelphia.

Entering the Latino World

Because HIV was so prevalent in the gay community, we focused our early energies on caring for men and were caught

31

unprepared when we received several requests for meals from Latino families in the summer of 1990. None of our initial group had strong relationships with the Latino community, and none of us spoke Spanish, so we did the obvious: we sought guidance from Latino leaders. They said, "Make your top priority food which is ethnically compatible." We were still relying on donated meals from restaurants so this meant we had to establish ties with Latino restaurants.

It was not hard to find restaurants willing to assist, but it took a few days to organize the necessary conversations with the owners and to ride out the perturbations associated with negotiating across the racial and cultural divide.

One family restaurant agreed to help, but the next day when we called to confirm the arrangement we were told the deal was off. This family had discussed MANNA's request during dinner while having a heated debate over an unrelated issue. This resulted in a divided opinion about whether to help MANNA. Fortunately, a week later the other conflict had subsided, and they called to say they would be pleased to donate some meals. During the next few months this family became a great friend to MANNA.

In another case the restaurant was owned by two brothers. On Tuesday, the first brother, Carlos, said yes, but the next day when we arrived to pick up the promised meals he was not there. The second brother, who ran the place alone on Wednesday, told us that he was opposed to everything Carlos did. "My brother is an idealist," he grumbled. "Carlos would give everything away. I hate having to watch out for the bottom line, but if we helped everyone who asked for handouts we'd be bankrupt."

We recognized the humanity represented in events like this and took them in stride. MANNA's requests seemed to flush out rather basic reactions: sometimes that led to trouble and sometimes to the releasing of people's goodness. We had agreed to treat any setback as a message to go about things in a different way, so we adopted a new approach. Henceforth we told the Latino restaurant owners that we'd become aware that there were families living with AIDS in their immediate environs and asked their counsel about how best to respond. The owners were much more invested when MANNA presented itself as seeking partners, and, of course, they had many more ideas than we did about how to sustain and nourish the families who had been their customers for years.

Finding Honor among the Drug Dealers

Many of the poorest Latino families lived in an economically devastated section of North Philadelphia. This barren stretch, once part of the city's vibrant industrial and manufacturing sector, had been abandoned by all save the drug dealers, who had made each street corner into a marketplace. While there were some users in the neighborhood, the dealers' main clients were drive-by whites who came from the suburbs, slipped off the arterial roads in their BMWs, mini-vans, or Broncos, made a quick purchase, and went on their way as if they were not participants in both the underground economy and the complex drug problems of urban America.

Our early visits to this neighborhood left us concerned whether MANNA's volunteers, most of whom were white and lived in downtown Philadelphia, would feel safe venturing into a place so foreign. The ideal was to get people living nearby to deliver the meals, but that would take time to organize, and when people are starving there is no time to waste. We resolved to get going right away. I decided to do the first week of deliveries to the three Latino families who had called. Then we'd know the risks and could figure out how to get these meals delivered and keep everyone safe.

My first call in this neighborhood was to some bricks and crumbling mortar that had once been a row house. All the houses on either side of it had been demolished, so it stood alone on a deserted block filled with abandoned cars. The place was lifeless. Not even a stray dog roamed the street. Huddled inside this decaying building was a young couple. Both were very sick.

I next visited the Hernandez family. Although they lived only three blocks away, the contrast was startling. As I pulled onto their street more than a dozen drug dealers swarmed around my car. Each had a marketing pitch designed for wealthy white consumers. Their energy gave the block a sense of vitality. I waved them off and carried my two bags filled with plastic and aluminum containers onto the porch of #517, leaving behind a trail of inviting odors emanating from the meals I had picked up from the restaurant twenty minutes earlier. As the grandmother at #517 invited me inside, I wondered if my car would still be there when I returned. Would there be a price to pay for venturing onto the drug dealers' turf and refusing to make a purchase? As I got caught up in meeting the Hernandez family, my anxiety about my car faded from consciousness.

Inside the Hernandez home, there was a festival of contradictory images. The house was spotless, and the dinner table had been meticulously set for ten people. There were several children under foot, and the whole home was awash with the joyful sounds of kids at play. Pedro, the man of the house, was the only one diagnosed with the virus. He no longer worked, and his wife was off earning the family income. Her mother, the grandmother to their three children, came each day to care for the needs of this home. In the mornings a brother and two sisters dropped off their preschool children for the grandmother to care for, while she kept an eye out for the special needs of Pedro. I had brought enough food for everyone. We had learned from Nora that parents with AIDS had few reserves, rarely had the strength to cook for their children, and would not eat until all their offspring were fed. So

MANNA had a firm policy: with families we delivered meals for the whole household. I momentarily wondered if this family genuinely needed MANNA's meals, a premature thought given that I knew nothing of their suffering.

I helped this vivacious grandmother set the meals on the table while she assembled her brood, including Pedro, who was wandering around the house in his swim suit, trying to stay cool. After holding hands in a family circle while they said a blessing in Spanish, I excused myself so I could make my next delivery.

As I went outside, I suddenly recalled my fear about what might happen to our family car. It was fine. No one had touched it.

The next day when I arrived with food for the Hernandez family, no drug dealers approached me. It was clear they had figured out what I was doing and had agreed to honor the purpose that brought MANNA onto their turf. Never again did a dealer approach me. Each noon, as I drove into their world, they waved to me warmly and assured me that no one would mess with my car. The drug dealers had appointed themselves as my protectors.

Fernando's Look

My last visit on that first day was to Maria's home. I already knew the HIV status of her family. Maria's oldest two, eleven and eight, were fine. They were born before she became infected. Her youngest two, however, Fernando and her eighteen-month-old, had been conceived after she'd contracted the virus and both were born HIV positive. (This was long before it was known that a woman's use of the AIDS drug AZT during pregnancy substantially lowered the probability of the newborn being infected.)

Maria lived on a busy block vibrating with children's energy. Her oldest two were among the scores of kids running through the water arch created by the fire hydrant, opened to cool off the neighborhood. Maria, one of the parents on the street looking out for the children's safety, recognized who I was long before I figured out who she was. Our initial exchange was brief. She pointed to her home and asked me to take the food and place it on the kitchen table. I was happy to oblige.

As I walked into Maria's home, my attention was drawn to the living room couch. There sat young Fernando, Maria's four-year-old son. He was just a month or two away from dying and was extremely weak. He could no longer sit up unaided. That day he was propped upright by a collection of pillows stuffed around his tiny frame. With a single glance I knew his whole existence had been defined by suffering. The only part of him that was a normal size was his head; since the virus had severely limited his body's growth, his head looked disproportionately large for his frame.

Fernando obviously knew why I was there. Without saying a word he gestured in the direction of the kitchen, but before I had a chance to move he had frozen me in place with a look that came from his soul. For ten or fifteen seconds, he held me in intense eye contact, and with his big brown eyes said thank-you to me in a way I had never experienced. Words can't describe what passed between Fernando and me that day. I felt this young lad who had experienced so much suffering all his life was speaking to me from his inner being and was reaching out to and communicating with my essence. Neither Fernando nor I said a single word to each other, but oh, what he said to me with those eyes! Never before had I seen such gratitude on the face of a human being.

Fernando's look redefined the meaning of thankfulness for me. This small boy, living out his final weeks in a body that had probably failed him every day of his young life, was exceedingly thankful for the small mercy of a good meal. In an instant, the image of his beautiful eyes was seared into my memory. I know it will be with me until my final breath and will serve as a perpetual reminder of how a small boy in the midst of intolerable suffering was able to be thankful.

Fernando was the first of Maria's family to die. It was late July. By Thanksgiving the toddler had also died. Maria, who was a single mother, managed to hang on for another two years, long enough for her oldest to reach his teens and her second to get into the sixth grade. Her two surviving children were among Philadelphia's first AIDS orphans.

We were still young in our experience with AIDS, but that summer we were inspired by what we found on the other side of what once was an ethnic divide for MANNA. We were also intrigued to be the beneficiaries of the basic goodness of drug dealers.

"Kids Care"

One of the first new members to join the MANNA board was a man bristling with energy and ideas. He was the producer of a radio show called *Kids Corner*, WXPN's daily call-in program for children, well known in Philadelphia for the wholesome ways it engaged youngsters in a wide range of issues. This radio executive was eager to involve MANNA in connecting children more fully to AIDS. However, this was a time of anguish for him as he watched friend after friend die, and needing a sabbatical from AIDS so his own heart could repair, he resigned from the board before his dream of building a MANNA-children link was realized.

He nevertheless continued to educate children about HIV on WXPN's call-in show, and in his own way he let his relationship with the kids of Philadelphia be a part of his own healing process. After one particularly successful talk show about AIDS, the kids were so fired up they asked how they could help. He floated with them the idea he had presented to the MANNA board a couple of years earlier: children creating artwork for people living with AIDS. The timing was right, and "Kids Care" was born.

Over the years MANNA built relationships with a wide range of organizations for a variety of reasons, but the one that touched me the most was Kids Care. It was so simple; it cost and produced no money, yet it enhanced the lives of everyone involved. This producer's dream had its seeds in his own grief and his commitment to foster honest dialogue among children.

Kids Care started in early fall and culminated during the holiday season. Children from local schools made special artwork as gifts for people living with HIV/AIDS. For a few weeks it was hung in a local gallery, and then each client was given a piece of artwork along with the special feast MANNA delivered on Christmas Day. In the process an exceptional partnership was created among Kids Corner, MANNA, several schools, and Woodmere Museum, a gorgeous mansion in the Chestnut Hill section of Philadelphia.

Patrick, MANNA's volunteer coordinator and director of public relations, described the event in the following way. "Each year it is kicked off when I and the director of education at Woodmere make visits to a number of public and private schools in Philadelphia, meet with art classes, and talk with them about HIV. Each class starts with a discussion of what the students know about AIDS, which is often quite extensive. For example, in one North Philadelphia fourth grade class, all the kids said they personally knew someone who had recently died of AIDS or who was ill with the virus at that time. These students are always full of questions and can talk about HIV in a matter-of-fact way.

"After talking about AIDS, the discussion turns to what it means to care for people who are ill, and I explain what MANNA does. Then the children brainstorm ideas, which leads to a number of projects that the students work on during the fall. By Thanksgiving the art is sent to Woodmere and for three weeks is hung on public display.

"The art teachers usually get the projects going, but once underway the energies of the students usually carry them. Some work in groups, others individually. Some teachers sus- pend their normal lessons to participate, while others include it seamlessly in the curriculum. Often parents who get to know about Kids Care call MANNA to ask how they can get their kids' classes involved."

In 1996, a dozen schools with diverse economic and ethnic backgrounds were involved with Kids Care. Students from grades one through twelve participated. When the art was hung in the gallery "it was like being in a garden filled with the energy and caring of kids," reported Woodmere's education director. "This is what I have been trying to create for our children at our gallery: wholeness and collaboration. I love the relationship between WXPN, Woodmere, and MANNA," she said. "We work well together and, when the host of Kids Corner, the favorite adult of Philadelphia children, shows up, the kids go crazy. I am also very pleased that Kids Care has shown so many young people how to get involved with AIDS."

The 1996 reception for the Kids Care artists was held on a rainy Sunday afternoon when museums everywhere were rec- ognizing "A Day without Art." To honor all who had died of AIDS, Woodmere like other participating galleries, had stripped its walls bare. Only the Kids Care exhibit was on display that day.

A graduate student from a nearby university whose first exposure to MANNA was the 1996 Kids Care reception described his experience:

"Many of the children had hooked up with classmates and were chasing each other around while feasting on the MANNA goodies that had been provided. Those without buddies wandered around trying not to feel embarrassed about being seen with their parents.

"The big attraction was a table of healing dolls, each brightly decorated to display the powers it possessed, with a piece of paper protruding from its side that described its powers and the artist's hopes about how the recipient would use them.

"Some students had made brightly colored stuffed animals that they called 'cuddly critters,' each with a card saying 'This Cuddly Critter was made with loving care. It needs lots of love and as many hugs as you can spare.'

"A class from a school in Northeast Philadelphia had made rag dolls and attached greetings like the following:

My name is Karen. My little present represents friendship. My flowers are a symbol of love. The feathers in my hair represent joy. The necklace and bracelet I am wearing represent happiness. I am wearing a lace skirt. It represents caring. I hope you enjoy being with me.

"The range of art the children created was spectacular. In addition to paintings of many kinds, colors, and sizes, there were some unusual and creative constructions. For example, one high school boy had made a water fountain out of a baking pan, copper pipes, a wok, some plastic tubing, and a small pump. Kids from Project Learn, in addition to setting up a loom with scraps of material for visitors to make a community weave, had created clay vessels filled with flowers and other cheerful items. One entry written in the book accompanying their pottery read:

This vessel will always remind you that not all people don't care. When you see this you will know that we care. Peace will follow you and your vessel wherever you go. Peace, love, and happiness always.

"A formal reception honoring the artists was held in a large room, built to display the art collection of the owner when Woodmere was a private home. The crowd was huge, so many of the kids sat on the floor up front. Then representatives of all the art classes were invited to come forward and tell a story about their projects.

"A couple of teachers spoke, but mostly it was the students. Those kids got to me. It was the simple human moments that were the most special. For example, one second-grader couldn't even get her head high enough to be seen above the podium. Before an adult could intervene, a ninth-grader raced forward, picked her up, and held her close to the microphone. 'AIDS is a real bad disease,' said this petite seven-year-old prophet, craning her neck so she could see over the lectern. Speaking in a strong voice, she continued, 'And I hope they find a cure someday. But we should not be afraid of people with AIDS because they are just like you and me.' Then she sat down as many an adult wiped away a tear.

"A third-grader said, 'Most of our time we do what the teachers tell us. With Kids Care we do what we like. It's fun to find out what you create when it comes from your heart.'

"One girl from the fifth grade read a poem she had written to go along with the clay cups, pots, and plates her class had made. These were her words:

> Slippery, silver clay,
> smooth against your fingers.
> Warm soap, hot tea with honey, cocoa.
> I made this pot for you,
> hoping it would be
> like sunshine against the sea,
> like pure river feelings,
> Silky waters and sand castles,
> like a funny bunny across green fields,
> like raindrops and wildflowers,
> like a big white fluffy cloud against purple skies,
> like dew drops floating in a dim mist.
> Sun, moon, stars,
> joy, joy and joy again.

"No matter how embarrassed the kids were while speaking, no matter how much they said or how eloquently or inarticulately they said it, each received a great round of applause."

After the children's artwork had been exhibited for three weeks at Woodmere, it was sent to MANNA, where volunteers wrapped each piece and sent it out with the special meal delivered on Christmas Day. Some children even got to present their own gift to a meal recipient by corralling their own family to be a MANNA meal deliverer on Christmas Day.

Volunteers reported over and over again during the ensuing months that they had seen the artwork proudly displayed somewhere in the person's room when they delivered meals. MANNA also received a pile of thank-you notes for these gifts, with heart-felt expressions of gratitude like the following: "This is the nicest gift I have ever received. I look at it every day. It cheers me up and makes me smile. The caring of children is so pure."

"Shut Up and Dance"

In 1992, the Pennsylvania Ballet was in financial crisis and had to close down. There was had no money to pay the performers. The dancers, desperate to keep ballet alive in Philadelphia, decided to keep dancing without pay. The community's response was unprecedented, and within a month $2 million was raised, due in large part to the support of the media. With this infusion of cash, our ballet company managed to survive.

The dancers wanted to do something to thank the community and elected to run a fund-raising event for some cause cherished by the people of Philadelphia. But they could not decide what to do. After days of arguing, someone finally yelled, "Let's just shut up and dance!" With that expression of frustration this event had its birth. "We knew how to dance," said the organizer. "What we had to offer the community was the gift of dance. We chose to raise money for AIDS because so many of our friends from the ballet world had died from this disease. We considered several possible beneficiaries and chose MANNA. Its mission was focused, simple, and tangible. Helping to feed people who are too ill to care for themselves seemed right for us. Also MANNA needed money desperately. So we went and met everyone at MANNA and built a strong friendship with them. Shut Up and Dance was born as a fund-raiser run entirely by the dancers. MANNA was invited to sit back and enjoy our gift."

The first year the dancers raised $1,400. They gave it all to MANNA. Within four years their gift from this event had grown to over $30,000. "Our first year it was a novice event," said one of the dancers, "but the community was so responsive Shut Up and Dance soon became a big production involving all kinds of contributors, from designers, to artists, to theater owners. We found sponsors to underwrite the event. If we had not done this the cost to produce it would have been prohibitive. People also made many in-kind contributions like printing and free use of space. Actually it was not hard to get donations and to raise money for such a cause. We even had to say no to some volunteers, like our mayor, who offered to do a dance for us while ceremonially opening the performance. That would have been the kiss of death! This event was also great for my colleagues and me. It gave us a unique opportunity to cut loose. The dancers did all the choreography, and we loved the chance to be creative, to express what was in our hearts.

"I grew to love MANNA," this dancer continued. "I began to volunteer, to deliver meals, to help prepare the food. All of us dancers think of ourselves as MANNA volunteers. We donate our time by dancing for MANNA. Most of all we identify with what MANNA does, the selfless acts of so many people. That's what draws me and the other dancers to MANNA.

It's a chance for us to give something to the community that gives so much to us."

Apart from the financial gift MANNA gratefully received from this annual performance we all felt wonderfully nourished by the dancers' emotional gifts. MANNA was uplifted by the poetry of these dancers, the generosity of their giving although they were in economic hard times themselves, and the creativity that flowed out of their own grief.

Once more we observed that gifts of insight, compassion, and encouragement were coming to us from those feeling exceedingly vulnerable. This was beautifully expressed by one of our volunteers after the second performance of Shut Up and Dance, back when the event was still small enough to be held in the Trocadero theater before an audience of only a couple of hundred.

"I often find my decisions fall unplanned into one another and bring me to an unexpected place. What happened on January 22 was such a journey. I had no patience at the thought of doing battle with the ice and the sliding and the mumbled curses. Staying huddled inside was my plan. But we had tickets for the Pennsylvania Ballet's Shut Up and Dance Benefit to honor MANNA's fourth anniversary.

" 'Forget it!' I said. 'Just think of the tickets as a donation.' My wife agreed, 'It's crazy!' 'Of course it could be interesting?' I said, hoping she would say yes and I could blame her for the pain of getting there. She knows me and returned, 'If you think so.'

"Sitting in the dark theater, looking at a bare stage, while the second ice age claimed the city I mumbled, 'Let's hope for the best.'

"The gods must enjoy the nimble way they move me around on the game board, because into the darkness came the voice of Aretha Franklin singing 'Johnny' while a man danced with an empty chair. And my heart was unlocked of memories.

"Whenever I help at MANNA my mind and spirit are

always on the meal and getting it out to the client, know-ing someone is waiting. But there in the dark, while a man danced, I remembered empty chairs.

"All around my table sit empty chairs of friends gone, my life diminished by their absence. I sat and watched this man move and caress his partner, his empty chair, while Aretha sang of words not spoken soon enough. 'Why did I wait till you were gone to remember you?'

"I saw a different MANNA that night. It's not just a meal and cheerful words; it's a place that honors the empty chair too. The dancer was dancing for me. Letting me return to my vault of memories, saying, 'Unlock it. Look at the sadness, too. It has a right to be seen.'

"I didn't realize I was crying until tears fell on my hands. That night, in the dark, while a man danced, all my friends sat around me and I heard old voices and smiled at remembered laughter. Even the ice was no longer an enemy. It was a part of the season. The cold and the dark had its place as much as the sun and the light. I inhaled all of it, and at the dance party after the ballet's performance I danced like never before.

"I had to. All my friends were watching."[4]

The Dance of Vulnerability

It is hard to deal with our vulnerability, be it personal, organi-zational, or communal. It can evoke our wish to hide. It can trigger our rage. It can prompt us to pretend we are strong. Rarely do we think of it as preparation for a period of renewal, as a time of gestation. Nor do we usually think of joining the ranks of the vulnerable to find answers to whatever ails us.

It is intriguing to consider what happened as a result of the vulnerability experienced by the Israelites who had carried only enough food to last one month.[5] This spoke to their ex-pectations. They thought thirty days should be enough time to get from Egypt to the promised land, from slavery to freedom.

It wasn't. By the forty-fifth day they were starving. Their despair was not just about hunger but the bleakness of the future. Before them was a gigantic and devastatingly barren desert. The prospect of finding food and water was zero, and they felt there was no chance they'd ever reach a destination even approximating the place they had left behind. Their dream of a land flowing with milk and honey had been replaced with a realistic anticipation of a brutal death.

They began to revolt. Moses and Aaron were the target of their enmity, but the real beef was with God, the One who had liberated them. For them seeing out the full measure of their days as slaves in Egypt seemed a better option than a life prematurely ended by malnutrition. For them, freedom was not worth the price!

Moses was distressed by their fickleness. He thought they had received plenty of proof that the Lord was their deliverer and that a few hunger pangs did not justify public panic. However, at this point Moses was still patient and forgiving. He advised them to direct their complaints to God. Moses suggested that being angry at God was okay. This man, who had been asked not only to find a new home for these escaped slaves but also to lead them into a new relationship with God as well seemed to be saying, "At least your anger indicates you are in some kind of relationship with the Almighty. It represents a start and I'm sure God will accept it."

His advice, to express the anger directly to the One making them feel weak, seemed to run counter to the way we humans are psychologically constructed. Imagine saying to a worker who feels crushed by a rigid and oppressive authority system, "Go to your tyrannical bosses and let them know how angry you are that their actions make you feel vulnerable." What's the likely response? "You've got to be kidding! Doesn't that make you even more exposed? Won't that make you an easier target in the future?" For most of us rage is the cue to circle the wagons, to keep the adversary at bay, to share our reality only with those who feel as we do, to rely solely on our own resources.

Moses counseled his congregation "to have it out with God and see where it leads you. If you take your vulnerability to the Lord, who knows what might happen?"

And what was God's response? Was it vindictiveness? Were they punished for their faithlessness?

No. They were sent the manna. For forty years they were given their daily bread. And in the process they were handed an important message, one as relevant today as it was a few thousand years ago. Our vulnerability is the inner soil in which can be planted the seeds that will ultimately bear the fruit needed to nourish the spirit.

Modern psychology, especially behaviorism, says be careful not to reward people when they are doing the wrong things, because that will encourage them to continue making the same mistake. Was God trying to ensure that the Israelites remain a collection of spiritual infants by rewarding them when they went astray? Would it not have been best to give them a pellet of food when they expressed their faith rather than their faithlessness? A behaviorist could be forgiven for thinking God got the Skinnerian reinforcement schedule mixed up.

But perhaps God was rewarding exactly the right thing. Was not the Almighty saying, "Bring your vulnerability to Me. And if, perchance, your anguish comes packaged as anger that's okay, for I can figure out that you are furious because you feel afraid. I can see the inner precariousness being masked by anger. And that's all right by Me. I will not punish you for being you. All I want is for us to be in relationship, and if this is a way you and I can remain connected, I'll take it!"

I can recall early in our marriage when I came home and some trivial thing my wife had done triggered my anger, which was really a release of the raw emotions my day at work had kicked up. She looked at me as if I'd come from another planet, and then as is her way, wrapped her arms around me until my sobbing heart, gridlocked by my attempts to freeze the tears I refused to release, could feel the love of a spouse who was able to see the vulnerability crammed within my angered facade.

God and my loving spouse both know how to dance with the child in me. Perhaps the boss cannot recognize that our anger is only the wrapping that hides the gift of our vulnerability. But God can and does.

Manna was one of many ways through which God's presence became known, not only to that first generation of wanderers, but to all peoples ever since. Which leads to a stunning question. Why was it to the lost and weary, the doubting and the cursing, the fearful and impoverished, that the Almighty gave this special revelation? Were there not others more worthy of this assurance?

A few thousand years later we have substantial evidence that many of the richest insights garnered by humanity have come from people overwhelmed by vulnerability, not only the Israelites of old as they wandered in the wilderness, but the Elie Wiesels and Deitrich Bonhoeffers trapped in Nazi prison camps, the African American slaves who gave rise to the freedom movement in the supposed land of liberty, Nelson Mandela languishing as a political prisoner on Robben Island during South Africa's darkest years, Mahatma Gandhi as he walked the earth in a pair of sandals and a loincloth telling the world that the end of colonialism was at hand. The list is very long.

Three

LEAPS OF FAITH

Lesson 3:
The leaps of faith we took
filled our spirits with vitality.

W E RECOGNIZED EARLY ON that for MANNA to get started we had to take some leaps of faith. Some were large; some were small. Some were personal; some were communal. Some were just beyond the bounds of rationality; some were so far out that logic was irrelevant. When MANNA began First Presbyterian Church was more attuned to God's absence than God's presence. The "Still Small Voice" was hard to discern amid the clashing sounds of sirens and city traffic rushing many to places they did not want to go. There was little music in our souls even though we had a magnificent choir. There was no prophet calling forth our noble selves, no dreamer speaking about a land of promise around the corner from our brokenness. We were so numb we barely recognized our barrenness. Doubt ruled.

MANNA's Leap of Faith

In 1990, when we used the rules of rationality to measure what we set out to do, how we were going to do it, whether we succeeded, we sounded crazy, even to ourselves. Our goal was to ensure that no person living with AIDS in Philadelphia ever went hungry again. Our modus operandi was to draw volunteers from the ranks of the indifferent, the under-resourced, and the overcommitted and to ask them to prepare and deliver daily, nutritious meals to those too ill to care for themselves. Our indicator of success was to be that the unloved and deserted felt cared for by the very community that had abandoned them. When people said we were "out of our minds" they were right. We were trying to move be-yond the confines of human reasoning and find a new way of thinking.

We were struggling with how to live on the boundary be-tween despair and hope, between order and chaos, between dream and reality, between doubt and faith, between rigidity and possibility.

MANNA's first leap of faith was our public commitment to feed, for free, every homebound person with AIDS for the rest of their days. The food would arrive hot and ready to be consumed, the portions would be sufficient to cover a person's nutritional needs for a whole day, and we would personally deliver it to wherever the person lived. We also committed ourselves to stand with, and work on behalf of, the AIDS community as long as the AIDS blight continued.

We made this commitment not knowing how many people would need MANNA's service, but the early projections were daunting. In 1990 it was estimated that thirty thousand people living in the Philadelphia area were HIV positive. How long most had been infected was unknown, but researchers guessed the incubation period before full-blown AIDS appeared was about ten years. Given the limitations of the medicine avail-able at that time, life expectancy was only another year or two. This meant that over the next decade as many as thirty thou-sand Philadelphians could die, an average of three thousand a year. If 10 percent of these individuals needed meals during the last year of their lives, MANNA could soon be deliver-ing to three hundred people daily. If the percentage requiring food were higher, more meals would be needed. Moreover,

HIV was continuing to evolve in ways that baffled everyone. No one knew the future of this virus, how large the demand for MANNA's services would be, or for how long.

Paul Tillich talks about faith being predicated on doubt.[6] If there is no doubt there cannot be faith, he reminded us. Well, we had doubt abundant. When MANNA made its initial commitment not one of us had a clue how we would carry it out, where the resources would come from, or who would do all the work. There were only seven of us involved at that point. We all had full-time jobs, and none of us was independently wealthy. The ravine separating promise from reality was so enormous that our choice was either paralysis or a leap of faith. We elected the latter path.

How did it all work out? In ways we could have never anticipated.

For a year and a half MANNA needed about $20,000 a month just to keep its head above water. We had a budget: in 1990 it was $200,000 for operations and $70,000 for start-up expenses; in 1991 it was a little over $300,000. The budget, however, had little impact on how we acted. We just did what was absolutely essential. We were as frugal as possible, cut every financial corner we could, wrote grant proposals to any foundation willing to accept a submission from us, and asked everyone we knew to help. There was quite a lead time for foundations to process grant proposals. Even those sympathetic to both our cause and our plight were clear it would be a year before we could expect a response. For us, looking a year ahead seemed pointless. Our need for money was right now.

Month after month we lived on the edge. No matter how little we tried to spend, the bills came to about $20,000. During the first year and a half we never once had any excess money. We started each month with just a few hundred dollars, expenses came stunningly close to $20,000, and the income we received matched expenses almost perfectly. This amazed us.

As board chair I was anxious about what to do the month when our income fell short of expenses. MANNA was too unstable for a bank to give us a loan. We had no track record and certainly could not foresee a point where we could catch up economically. I decided to take out a line of credit on my family home, figuring that might help keep MANNA afloat for a few months should we hit a crisis. Not once, however, did I need to draw on that emergency account to tide MANNA over. From January 1, 1990, until the end of my term as board chair in 1996, there was not a single month that MANNA did not have the cash to pay its bills. And with the exception of one anomaly, an isolated incident, not a single person asking for MANNA meals went unfed. By the end of 1996, MANNA had served close to half a million meals, there were 650 volunteers working weekly, and we had a budget in excess of a million dollars.

How did this happen? I still marvel when I think about it. People from everywhere began to help. In came a check for several thousand dollars from a man sending MANNA the profits from his weekend sidewalk sale. In came a check for $36.27 from the children in the sixth grade of a local school, the proceeds of their fall bake sale. In came a check for $2,500 from the gay men's bowling league from a fund-raiser they had run especially for MANNA. In came a check for $10 from a sixty-year-old man, his birthday gift from his aging mother. Somehow the money began to arrive. Never enough to quiet our anxious hearts, but always enough to pay that month's bills.

Meanwhile a growing cadre of MANNA friends mobilized at a high speed to put a substantial fund-raising program together. This was led by one volunteer who was dedicating more energy to MANNA than we ever imagined any individual could donate. By the end of the eighteen-month period during which we needed $20,000 a month but had no reserves, we started to have substantial fund-raisers of our own.

Our first art auction netted $45,000. Foundations like the Pew Charitable Trusts, having concluded that MANNA had stability and promise, committed $30,000 a year. This change was a relief, because at that point the demand for our services began ballooning. MANNA's expenses were growing unpredictably, and $20,000 a month was no longer sufficient.

One day more than all others we felt the presence of an invisible hand. David, who had recently become our second executive director, was having a hard time living with the anxiety associated with our precarious financial situation. MANNA's treasurer and I were trying to calm him down, actually "scrape him off the ceiling," was how we described it to each other. David was beside himself. Substantial monies that had been promised were going to be delayed for months. To make things worse, the board had just approved a 40 percent increase in the budget for the following year. It was the middle of December, and if we received every cent we hoped might come in before year's end, MANNA was still going to be $35,000 short in 1994.

David knew of MANNA's hand-to-mouth existence and when he became executive director a few months earlier he had made it a major goal to create a financial steady state. The board had been impressed with David's expertise and his enthusiasm to create monetary reserves. However, the treasurer and I had been through enough to know that our new executive director's initiation into the realities of MANNA's cash flow would be a bumpy road. David had just hit his first big pothole. He was angry with someone who had just betrayed him; I don't recall whom, and it doesn't matter. He felt like a failure and, as the new kid on the block, was upset about letting us old-timers down. In the next room, Emma, a soul-filled staff member who had been involved in every big and small moment of MANNA's life and could no longer be surprised by anything, heard the muffled screams coming from David's anguish. She felt for him but was privately smiling about the induction that all who deal with MANNA's finances ultimately go though.

The treasurer and I knew that the best we could do at this time was to assure David that if we were $35,000 in the hole for the year it was not his fault, that MANNA had endured rough financial times before, and that we would get through this, although we could not answer his pleading question "How?"

Two days later I received a phone call from David. "Kenwyn, you won't believe what just happened?"

"What?" I asked relieved by the substantial shift in his tone.

"A stranger just walked in through the door and said he wanted to make a gift to MANNA. I said, 'Thank you. But who are you? And do you wish to write a check today?' He said, 'I am the executor of an estate. A man who recently died asked that everything he had be left to any Philadelphia AIDS organization I thought worthy. I have chosen MANNA and would like to write you a check right now.' "

David continued breathlessly, "I was grateful, Kenwyn, but frankly I was expecting a few hundred dollars. When he handed me the check I couldn't believe it. It was for exactly $35,000. I'm calling to tell you we met budget this year after all!"

All I could think of saying was "Welcome to MANNA, David!"

The Meal Recipients' Leap of Faith

Equally important were the leaps of faith taken by those who asked for MANNA's help. Most of the people we served were independent souls who had cared for themselves since becoming adults. To place a call and say to MANNA, "I need help," represented a leap of faith and took courage. They were saying, "I put my life in your hands. You promise to care for me. I accept." When calls came into MANNA asking for food, they were usually placed by people who could no longer care for themselves, whose savings were spent, and who had no companion or family to help out. They might be suffering from uncontrollable diarrhea, struggling for breath, fighting recurring pneumonia, or dealing with the loss of eyesight. That was usually a hard phone call to make, for it was the final admission that they could no longer care for themselves, a very humbling statement, one that takes away the last vestiges of self-respect. Saying to a stranger, "I place my life in your hands and ask you look after me as best you can," represented a final letting go.

No words can describe what it felt like to receive a call from a crackling voice saying, "My name is Fred; I need MANNA meals," code for "I am electing to trust MANNA with the thing I value most, my life." A few minutes later the phone would ring again and another frail voice would say the same thing. The phone would ring again, and again, and again. It was Bill, then Joan, then Natashia all saying "I trust you to care for *me*."

The trust offered by the meal recipients was clear and honest. By the time they called most were in the end stretch and were reaching out for a lifeline. Our collective heart was touched whenever people asked for our help, and somehow their willingness to depend on us augmented our dependability.

One MANNA volunteer described her experience: "When Steph and I first became parents, emotions were born in me I did not know even existed, emotions for which a vocabulary has yet to be invented. I felt we had been given a sacred trust, one rooted in the totality of our baby's neediness. Her faith in us was unreasoned and unreasonable. She trusted because that is what babies do. It was as spontaneous as the air that filled her lungs at birth. She had no agenda, no guile, no scheme, no plan for reciprocity. That's the kind of trust people place in MANNA, and in the process they teach us what trust means."

As a person came to the end of life, the act of trusting like
a child was initially hard. It had the quality of regressing to
an earlier state, which provoked the widest range of emotions.
One day when the MANNA volunteer came to visit, Altman
described his experience:

"I've had this awful virus for ten years. I worked as an
accountant until I got pneumonia and had to quit. I live in
Center City. My apartment is small, but it's all I need. It has
a great view of the city, which helps me stay connected to
the world. I made plenty of money and spent it on fancy cars,
the theater, and expensive dinners. Most of my friends lived
around here too, until they started dying.

"As you can see, I don't tidy up much," he said pointing to
his bed, books piled in milk crates all around the walls and a
TV, VCR, cassette player and tapes bundled on top of each
other. "Notice how perfectly organized my desk is, though.
That's where I keep my medicines. I have many bottles I must
keep track of, so I have them arranged like business files.

"I've lost a lot of weight, don't have much hair left, and
am just a skeleton now. It's the chemotherapy. They've been
treating me for lymphoma. I'm now taking too much medicine. It does me no good. Before I got pneumonia the only
medicine I took was AZT. I did that because my partner, a
nursing student, thought it was good for me. My partner has
died, but I still take it for his sake. The AZT doesn't help but
it doesn't hurt either.

"My doctors believed protease inhibitors would be good for
me. I took them from March until August, until I got gravely
ill and they discovered my lymphoma. I hate the chemotherapy and all the medications. Chemo makes me bald, gives me
mouth ulcers, and makes me vomit constantly. My body is
rejecting the therapy. However, the lymphoma is disappear-
ing, so it must be helping. But I don't like it. I prefer herbal
therapies and my healing circle.

"Many of my friends have died from AIDS. Brian first, then

Bill, then John, then Kenny.... The list is too long, twenty-seven in all. That's a lot of friends to have die, and I'm only forty-two. Many of their deaths were awful. It's best not to dwell on it, but it's hard not to when it's the most significant thing happening to you.

"Thankfully my family and my friends have been supportive. When I first was diagnosed, I told only one person. It was so different ten years ago. I was ashamed, embarrassed, and scared. The firm where I was working was very closed-minded. I thought I would lose my job, not only because of the HIV but because of my lifestyle. So I was secretive about everything. Attitudes are changing. People are getting more educated. The stigma is not quite as bad. The worst part now is being sick. Some days I sit and do nothing. I feel lethargic, which makes me even sicker.

"I began receiving MANNA meals a year ago. I've known about them a long time. I live near the church where MANNA started, and many friends, including my partner, got MANNA's meals. If I didn't have MANNA I would have to shop and cook for myself. That would be too difficult now. I have a great time with Beth, who delivers on Thursdays, and Carol, who delivers on Tuesdays and Fridays. They both stay and chat. It's nice. Beth is in the theater, so we talk about that. Some volunteers just come and drop off the meal, and that's fine too. But it is special when Beth and Carol visit. As for the quality of the food — my chemotherapy has killed my taste buds so I'm a poor judge of what's good any more.

"It is best if the deliveries come when you expect, but I understand that each day volunteers' schedules change and they deliver during their lunch hour, so it is difficult. Plus, the sheer number of deliveries is awesome. It is impossible to drop off everyone's meals at noon. MANNA provides a service that fulfills a need I have, and I am very thankful."

Over and over MANNA volunteers have reported how much they have found the courage to embrace the fullness of their own lives, with all its unique contours, as a result of the encounters they have had with people like Altman. Sharing time with those who day after day, week after week, month after month have had to mobilize immense courage to squeeze the possibilities out of the hour at hand was inspiring. We learned that one does not have to go the temple, to the ashram, to the mosque, to the church, to find inspiration. It can be found in the back allies, in the dark corners, in the cracks in the walls.

The Donors' Leap of Faith

Another group who showed us how to take leaps of faith was MANNA's donors.

All who belong to community organizations know what it is like to support the financial needs of the institutions of which we are a part. However, this giving occurs in an established system of relationships with an explicit or implicit reciprocity. We know the institution, and the institution knows us. We get something from our church, play reading group, school, synagogue, football club, or mosque, and it seems reasonable to financially support that which nourishes us.

Giving to organizations like MANNA is quite different. Donors contribute to a cause they carry in their hearts but from which they will never receive any services themselves. Further, the only relationship they have with the organization can be the mailing of a check. They rarely know if their money does anything of value or just sustains the organization's structure.

Today, in the United States, many organizations make claims on our charitable giving, from UNICEF to the neighborhood Boy Scout troop, from Save the Children to the volunteer fire department, from famine relief in Africa to the homeless shelter nearby, and we needed to know why people chose to give money to MANNA. So we interviewed a number of donors and asked them. Virtually all said their giving to MANNA was catalyzed by the loss of someone special due to AIDS. Their dominant response was that they opened their wallets as a way of opening their hearts. Their giving was a part of their grieving. All spoke of their gifts to MANNA in passionate terms.

When MANNA received a donation it was not money we were being given, but a broken heart wrapped in dollar bills. Our donors were first and foremost giving us their hearts and asking us to help them deal with their own brokenness.

It takes strength to acknowledge that one has a broken heart, and it takes courage to then give a piece of that brokenness away. Usually when we feel broken we hope others can give us something that will make us whole. It is not part of social orthodoxy to give away that which we most want for ourselves. However, that was what our donors said they were doing. They gave to MANNA their brokenness and asked us to do something with it. We were startled to discover this, but on reflection it made sense. They were doing the same as the rest of us, just in a different form.

Over the years I have noticed that when everything was going well for me, when I had all I needed, I was far less generous than when my tears were close to the surface and my heart was aching. I don't mean more generous with my money, although that was true too. I mean more generous with the self I offered to others. Ironically I've been more prone to give of myself when I was unsure about the value of that self. Of course, it turned out the self shared was of greater value to others than the self withheld.

The words of Craig, a donor, captured both the leap of faith many donors took by giving to MANNA, and how they discerned whether their trust was justified.

"I am a filmmaker and love my career, but I hate that all my international travel makes it impossible to be more involved with MANNA. This is an organization I know about because

I have many friends who have been affected by this disease.
It was my sadness that prompted me to give to MANNA.
I have been contributing since MANNA was located in the
church basement. I identify with its mission, respect what it
does, and admire the reputation it has developed. MANNA is
well run and effective. It makes the hard decisions. It says no
when it has to, something many non-profit organizations will
not do — setting boundaries and holding staff, volunteers, and
clients accountable to set criteria. MANNA does this in a way
that is respectful of all. And it responds compassionately. For
example, if a client is not there when the meal is delivered and
has not told anyone about the absence beforehand, the service
is suspended. As soon as the client calls the service is restored
right away. This is one way MANNA tries to keep everyone
being responsible. I have complete faith in MANNA. Those
people are handling love, since at MANNA food equals love.
When you are around that much love it is hard to mismanage
it. I expect I will always donate to MANNA. If I were out
of work or did not have any money to help I would give
MANNA my time. I get so much from giving, to not do so
would be to deprive myself."

The Leap of Faith Concept

The Exodus narrative indicates that the Israelites had to take
numerous leaps of faith, many of which occurred on the
journey from Egypt to the promised land. Søren Kierkegaard
elegantly described this leap of faith.[7] According to Friedman,
Kierkegaard's leap of faith meant letting go of the very things
we cling to most.[8] Then, by a process we cannot compre-
hend, we discover that the act of relinquishing brings back
the very thing that was so painfully released, except it re-
turns transformed. Henceforth it no longer has to be grasped
to be retained, for it is eternally there. The decoupling must
be real. One must truly relinquish it. Kierkegaard illustrated

with Abraham's response when God told him to offer up his beloved son, Isaac, as a sacrifice. Friedman describes how we might react to this request of God: "You've got to be kidding! After all we've been through. You, who so tried my patience I even took my wife's handmaiden who bore me Ishmael! For my lack of faith You rebuked me harshly, but still You promised that Sarah would bear me a son. Then came the gift of Isaac, but now You ask that I offer him as a sacrifice, to actually slay him!" Abraham did not argue as most of us would, but took his son, placed him on the altar and prepared to kill him. He was going to do it. He was actually going to sacrifice his child.[9]

Abraham did not ask why he was to make this sacrifice. He just raised his knife to do what was asked of him. Abraham let go of everything a reasoning mind would find acceptable and relied entirely on faith. Then by some absurd process he recovered what he surrendered.

Kierkegaard argues that to find ourselves one must surrender the self to that which is beyond the self. In a place beyond place, in a time beyond time, in a Self beyond the self, we discover that we are part of an existence that is greater than ourselves. However, we can glimpse this only when the self is quenched. The bind is that our knowledge of this beyondness is both made possible by and limited by our human self. If we did not have a self, we could not lose it; if we could not lose it we could not know that there is a Self from which the self springs; if we could not catch a fleeting glimpse of this Self, the very concept of self would lack meaning.

Abraham's willingness to risk all led him to discover that love given away grows and comes back greatly magnified. It is hard to recognize that we are made whole by that which tears us apart. We mortals understandably cling to what we have acquired, protect ourselves from losing what is in short supply, and seek assurances that any sacrifice we make will bring us just rewards. Alas, we cannot reason our way into believing. Our only option is to leap, in the face of all the absurdity. That's what makes it faith.

The lessons discovered by Abraham were not easily transferred to later generations. This was not "one small step for man, one giant leap for mankind." The offspring of this giant of faith had some very hollow spiritual times. One of Abraham's twin grandsons, Jacob, with his mother's help, stole the birthright from his brother by duping his aged and blind father, Isaac, the very man who, as a boy, had been the one Abraham was willing to sacrifice. Then Joseph, the dreamer, Abraham's great grandson, simply because he was the apple of his father's eye, was sold into slavery by his brothers. These siblings were the product of Jacob's bizarre relationship with his two wives, Leah and Rachel, his first cousins, the warring sisters, and their two handmaidens. If there were psychologists back then they might have labeled this a dysfunctional family.

It was these offspring of Abraham, many generations later escaping slavery in Egypt, who were sustained by manna while wandering in the wilderness. Over and over again Moses tried to educate them to get them up to speed, but they wanted nothing of it. They just longed for the barrenness to be behind them, but they doubted they would ever escape the horrors of the desert. They railed against their existence, accused Moses of being a poor leader, and cursed God for His absence. Only when they surrendered to their plight did they discover God was nearby.

In many ways MANNA lived at the vortex of both a blessing and a curse. The curse? So many people being snatched from the prime of life. The blessing? The emergence of a community of caring, discovering anew what the human heart could do when infused with spirit. MANNA members often noted that the intense juxtaposition of both the blessing and the curse and our willingness to ride the unpredictable ebbs and flows of our clients' lives gave our organization its vitality. As we set out to deliver a meal we never knew if we were about to encounter the specter of death or a scene in which pain and anguish had momentarily slipped into the background and the joy of life was occupying center stage. Volunteers were right when they insisted that MANNA's strength lay in its connection to those we served, that in its heart and soul MANNA was a client-driven organization.

MANNA's greatest anguish was that it constantly lived a hand-to-mouth existence. For years, this organization hovered on a precarious edge, forced to focus solely on the present. We could not afford more than a moment to celebrate any achievement because there were always another few hundred hungry people needing to be fed. We had to stay focused on today and be willing to let tomorrow take care of itself. If we focused too much on the demands of the future, today would be lost and then tomorrow would be irrelevant.

No one ever planned to build an organization based on a moment-by-moment, day-by-day, week-by-week ethos. It just happened. The many attempts we made to get beyond this only gave us enough slack to deal with the crisis just around the corner. None of us liked this, but it was our reality: for MANNA to stay alive every today required as much commitment as yesterday. And this proved to be a *mitzvah.* In a strange and wonderful way there was a kind of parallelism between our organizational life and the life of each person living with AIDS. The same precariousness, the same uncertainty about what each day might bring, the same anxiety about how long life as we knew it might last, provided a bond between MANNA and its clients. It kept us collectively in harmony with the daily reality of those we served.

It also seemed that, by some process we never fully grasped, MANNA managed to tap something tucked away in the core of each of us, a hunger for faith. If, as Tillich says, faith is really possible only in the midst of doubt and ceases to be viable when we stand on the rock of certitude, then could it be that the depth of our doubt made us open to the faith of the ages? Certainly AIDS shoved us all, the sophisticated and naive alike, into the void where doubt and uncertainty resided. There, in the place where hopelessness was total, we gave up even hoping and were exposed to our raw hunger for faith. That craving built and built until in the midst of total absurdity we just ended up jumping. Why did we take the plunge? Because we could not think of anything else to do. We were at the end of our rope. Rationality had deserted us. The only thing left was to act out the absurd. It was that leap that released the ever-flowing springs at the bottom of the wells of our despair. When we went through the door and looked at the world with differently calibrated eyes we saw that the whole landscape was covered with manna. In the face of our own impoverishment, in the fullness of our limitations, we found the abundance that gives life to life.

Four

THE STRENGTH OF VULNERABILITY

Lesson 4:
MANNA's vulnerabilities were its strengths,
and its strengths were its vulnerabilities.

B Y 1996 MANNA had 650 volunteers working weekly, an enormous number of helpers. These volunteers brought their labor, their anxieties, their energies, their wish to be healed, their grief, their craziness, their essence. We loved them, felt nourished by them, and occasionally were infuriated by them.

The Volunteers: MANNA's Lifeblood

While volunteers were MANNA's greatest strength, it took energy to have that strength be realized. They came from every corner of the city. Some ran major corporations; others were unemployed. Some were full-time homemakers; others were but a welfare check away from being homeless. Some were in the prime of life; others would soon become MANNA clients themselves.

Volunteers worked at MANNA during their leisure time, and hence often wanted to relax a little and hang out with newfound friends. However, for the staff there were always many things to be done, and dealing with some volunteers required patience and understanding. The staff had to take volunteers on their own terms and give each individual a way to find his or her own place in the organization. Despite the energy it took to integrate volunteers, this labor pool was a great asset, not just because it was free, but also because it had a totally different character from paid labor.

It took us a while to see this, but as Steve, MANNA's distribution coordinator for numerous years, constantly reminded us, "Volunteers are also MANNA's clients. They come through our doors with emotional and spiritual needs that also require feeding. The beauty is that these souls are nourished by feeding others."

Once a volunteer was assigned to a part of MANNA's operation, either the chef or the distribution coordinator had to integrate that person into the operation. Some inductions went easily; others were complex. Of course, experienced volunteers and clients were crucial in teaching newcomers. We were always touched when we heard stories like that of Trevor, handled so skillfully by Lou, the client.

Trevor's First Day

"I was anxious about my first delivery. I was afraid I would not know what to do, having never met anyone with AIDS who was really ill. Steve [the distribution coordinator] told me not to worry, 'because I'm sending you to Lou. He will help educate you,' he said reassuringly. 'Lou is a fifty-year-old in South Philly who was once a furniture manufacturer. He was diagnosed in 1988 and is comfortable talking about anything. He's received meals for two years. Spend a little time with him. You'll learn a lot.'

"I decided to call before I arrived to check that he was home and to tell him I was a first-time MANNA deliverer. He thanked me for calling and made me feel at ease by first asking if I was allergic to cats. This was so thoughtful. Here I was taking food to a really sick man, and he was concerned about my well-being. It was easy talking to him, even on the phone.

"He lived in an old, run-down apartment that sat atop a beer distributor. On one side of the street there were old row houses, while on the other side there were boarded-up buildings that had once been small factories. It was predominantly an Italian community with a significant number of African Americans.

"Lou, a balding man with a circle of gray hair around his head and five rings on his left ear, greeted me at the door. He had no front teeth, but he put them in when we got upstairs. To get to his apartment we climbed a narrow, dimly lit staircase. The building was old and had a musty smell. The hallway was so narrow he had to squeeze past me to open the door.

"In contrast to the darkness in the hall, the apartment was light and had many nicely framed pictures, hung with care. He had a beautiful glass-topped table with black lacquered chairs that fit snugly into a small dining area. There were knickknacks all over the place, which I was sure had stories behind them because of the careful way they were displayed. An avid collector myself, I know what fun it is to talk about how they were acquired. We spent a long time discussing where he had found his prize pieces. Most of them had come from garage sales or flea markets.

"Lou was thin, but looked healthy. He had been introduced to MANNA by his lifelong partner, who also got meals before dying in 1993. 'My partner was devastated when he learned I had the virus too,' Lou said. 'For a long time I refused to be tested. One day, back when I was working and before I knew I had HIV, I went to the health service at work to get them to check out a rash on my leg. They took tests and then told me I had psoriasis and gave me some ointment. However, before I left they matter-of-factly said I had tested HIV positive. That was it. No counseling. Just the hard, cold, brutal reality!' Lou said he had suspected all along that he had AIDS, and this confirmed his worst fears.

"Lou was embarrassed to admit that he had unprotected sex but talked at length about the importance of monogamy. He wanted me to know that he did not contract HIV by having indiscriminate sex.

"Lou continued to work but often had to call in sick because of the side effects of the medications. He finally decided to tell his boss he had HIV and said he was willing to resign. His boss insisted he stay but wanted to call a meeting of his co-workers to tell them about Lou's illness. Lou said, 'I didn't object but refused to attend the meeting. I didn't want to see their faces. I knew many of them were homophobic and objected to my lifestyle. One day I cut my hand and everyone ran in the other direction when they saw me bleeding. I tried to bandage it myself, but I needed help. Someone did finally assist me. When I thanked him I assured him that I understood why he'd been reluctant to help.'

"Lou seemed so calm and patient handling this situation, so understanding and forgiving. I asked whether this was his general temperament, or if he felt he had to model good behavior on behalf of all being stigmatized because of AIDS. He replied, 'By nature I'm forgiving, but I do feel compelled to act in ways that do not increase the intolerance of others toward people with AIDS.'

"Lou was effusive about MANNA's food and how it was presented, which he thought reflected our respect for the dignity of those we served. I suddenly felt proud to be part of this organization.

"We talked at length about his isolation. 'Many of my friends have died,' he said, 'and many others have lost so many loved ones they began to shy away from me because it was too tough to deal with my being sick as well. I've become a loner. I now rely on my cats for companionship. Many old friends don't visit or call anymore.' Lou was not bitter about this. He understood.

"His isolation was why MANNA became so important to him. The daily visits were a comfort because they helped him fight being reclusive. Lou said his interactions with MANNA deliverers had been mostly good and the bulk of the time he experienced what he called a 'giving attitude.' He illustrated by describing Monday and Tuesday as his favorite days 'because the delivery person always takes time to talk with me. Sometimes they seem afraid to touch me when they are giving me the food. I understand why, so it's okay. It takes courage to bring us these meals.'

"As I left Lou, I felt both sad and uplifted. My original anxiety about delivering meals for MANNA had gone, but I wondered how the volunteers deal with all the sadness. I called Steve and thanked him, and he assigned me to be Lou's Wednesday person. I phoned Lou to tell him this. Lou was so kind. 'Now I will have good days on Monday, Tuesday, and Wednesday,' he said. That's how MANNA entered my life."

The Blessings and the Struggles of the Volunteer Labor Pool

As an organization MANNA was vulnerable on many fronts, but none more acute than its complete reliance on a volunteer labor force. This was well captured by Tunga, one of our kitchen volunteers.

"MANNA seems highly organized. The place is usually crowded, and there are people going in many directions at the same time. Each day we volunteers work hard on a few small tasks, and by nightfall every person with AIDS in Philadelphia in need of food has been fed. That's amazing. We also have fun doing it.

"My shift has six males and me, an Asian woman. One man

is African American, one is from Argentina, and the rest are white Americans. Our ages range from twenty to forty, except for one who is retired. We get along well and have a lot of energy, especially the Argentinean who has a superb singing voice. He keeps us perpetually entertained. His 'Don't Cry for Me, Argentina,' is awesome. Sometimes I try to speak Spanish with him, despite my limited vocabulary, but usually we end up chatting in French, which we both enjoy. The most inspiring part of being at MANNA is seeing a blind woman who is often there folding and mailing MANNA's newsletters.

"However, MANNA is always vulnerable, given its reliance on volunteer labor. One day I was unable to make my kitchen shift. When I had called the previous morning to ask if I could come some other time, the man answering the phone asked me to call back later. They were in a crisis. I heard panic in his voice. Only one kitchen worker had showed up that morning and all the staff were running around trying to get the food cooked, packaged, and ready for delivery."

Managing the volunteer labor force was MANNA's most delicate dance. We always needed enough workers, but not too many. We had to be able to make good use of everyone's contributions but not overtax them. We had to keep all the volunteers deeply connected to MANNA's primary purpose and responsive to its policies but not cramp their style or their individual creative urges. We had to be gracious when someone we counted on could not make it at the last minute.

MANNA had a full-time volunteer coordinator, Patrick, who was gifted at recruiting, inducting, training, managing, and calming our volunteers. He came to MANNA early in its history, helped our organization grow, and rode through every pothole we hit. As he pointed out, "There were some naturally occurring events which were great recruiting occasions, such as major holidays when the media approached us for a special interest story. Advertisements for volunteers worked well at these times. But the publicity was a two-edged sword. We often got more helpers than we could use. That meant some people had to be put on a waiting list until a slot opened. You can't recruit people and then say 'we can't use you right now.' On other occasions we got many new helpers, but the extra visibility of MANNA attracted an unexpected influx of clients, which set off a cycle of needing even more volunteers.

"Maintaining a balance between the number of clients and the number of volunteers was complex," said Patrick. "MANNA's policy was to never turn away a client. Hence the cushioning had to be built into the volunteer end, which required patience and understanding, something that, fortunately, MANNA people had in spades."

MANNA had low volunteer turnover, for which we were grateful. We structured our volunteer activities in bite-sized chunks, which prevented people from getting stretched too thin, but each person could do as much as he or she chose. Also, preparing and delivering meals was relatively easy, took little effort, and we all sensed the difference we were making to people's lives. This was especially true for the drivers who interacted with the clients. Many were so moved by these encounters they built significant relationships with the clients, taking them out to dinner, helping them move to new housing, and in some cases even being present as they died.

There were times, however, when we had to ask a volunteer to leave. That forced us to address the complex question of what constitutes justifiable grounds for dismissing a volunteer. It was straightforward if a person deliberately refused to do what was best for clients, but there were many gray areas.

MANNA's policy was to welcome all, including those who didn't know how to manage their feelings about people who were different from them. We tried to give everyone the time to adjust to each other and to grow into new understandings of themselves and others, but if some emotional shifts did not occur we had to take action. Once a young man refused to work beside a woman because she was openly lesbian. He had to be told, "Because MANNA includes everyone you are expected to accept others who are different from you. We will help you all we can, but if you can't or won't change your attitudes, you will need to find another outlet for your volunteer energies." While adopting a policy of tolerance toward all, we were clear that we would reject those unwilling to be tolerant.

We were troubled by such paradoxes but were too busy to worry about them much. Ultimately we decided to accept the whole range of ironies associated with doing this work. But each time we banged into one of these emotionally charged organizational cul-de-sacs we were whiplashed into taking actions that were disquieting.

Sometimes getting volunteers to act in a consistent manner was complex. The following story illustrates the difficulty. Anna was a sixty-year-old Puerto Rican woman. For years after getting the virus she cooked for herself. Then a fire destroyed her kitchen. She was given some money by the government, but one day her food stamps were unexpectedly cut from $148 to $54 per month. Desperate, she called MANNA. The next day we started sending her meals. After six months Anna suddenly stopped getting MANNA meals. She was understandably upset.

When Steve, our distribution coordinator, investigated what had happened, this was what he reported finding. "Anna had a twelve-year-old grandson who lived with her. He was in the seventh grade, and most days was in trouble at school. He was forever fighting with other boys. Anna was always receiving calls from his teacher to tell her the latest ruckus he had started. In an attempt to intervene Anna tried to go to the school each lunchtime to check up on her grandson. That's when most of the fights occurred. Anna's anxiety was extra high because her daughter had been shot and killed a few years earlier. She felt it was her job to keep her dead daughter's son safe.

"When Anna left her house she taped a note on her door asking the MANNA deliverer to put the food inside the storm door. All the deliverers, except our Monday driver, were willing to do this. He refused because it was against MANNA policy. It so happened that everyone except our Monday man had formed a relationship with Anna and knew why she was absent, that she would soon return, and hence made the discretionary decision that leaving the meal as she asked was okay.

"This was how Anna described her experience of the volunteers," said Steve. " 'The lady who delivers on Tuesdays is nice. She comes inside to talk and even brought me cushions for my kitchen chairs. The Wednesday and Thursday people are nice too. One brought Halloween candy for my grandson, and another brought a cake on his birthday. The man on Friday is always late. He doesn't get here until three, but he calls to tell me he is still coming. Saturday two girls from the university bring my food. They are all nice, and I look forward to their visits. Except the man who comes on Monday.'

"Our Monday deliverer had no interaction with Anna and knew little about her life. He felt compelled to do exactly what he'd been instructed: 'Never leave the food if no one is there, then call the distribution coordinator right away.' Following policy guidelines, I automatically suspended Anna's meals until she called. The reason for this rigid policy, of course, is to preserve food safety. If hot food is left out too long, it spoils and then it is a health hazard, especially for a person ill with AIDS. Then our clients are made sick by the very food being sent to sustain them."

Situations like this took a lot of staff energy to unravel, and in this case it was made extra hard by the fact that Anna spoke little English. It was often not possible to send volunteers fluent in Spanish, and Steve, our distribution coordinator, spoke no Spanish. Hence he had to find a translator to be on the phone whenever he talked with her. Anna's meals were recommenced immediately, but instead of the food being left behind the screen door when she was out, it was delivered to a neighbor's place. That way both the food's safety could be preserved, and Anna could get her meals.

Another big difficulty MANNA faced was reliance on certain groups of people. College students contributed a great deal, but their energies had to be replaced when they went home for the summer or during semester breaks or exam week. Events like the Jewish high holidays came dangerously close to crippling MANNA a few times.

But all these were merely managerial problems we had to deal with and on balance were trivial in contrast with what the volunteers brought.

Rachel's Delight

MANNA's building was always full of boundless energy, and we were perpetually thankful for the whole range of people who gave themselves to this work, people like Rachel, whose enthusiasm simply couldn't and shouldn't be contained. This was how she characterized her time at MANNA.

"I have a young family and a job and juggle many things, like getting the children to Hebrew classes and sports practices. For me caring for others is part of my identity as a Jewish woman. *Tzedakah,* serving others, is a tenet of our faith, and making meals for others, particularly those with AIDS, is a *mitzvah.* Six of my Thursday morning crew are Jews, and we share something special.

"I learned about MANNA because my best friend's lover received MANNA meals. Both of these men have since died of AIDS. I began to volunteer at MANNA because I wanted to be around people who knew what was going on. While working in the kitchen I think about the meals we are making as being for someone else's best friend. Many of the volunteers at MANNA in my age group have a similar personal connection to AIDS. That's what led us to become volunteers.

"I first volunteered in the kitchen on Tuesdays but only lasted a month. This group was well behaved, cliquish and did not fit someone like me. They went out for fancy little lunches together. That's not my style. A staff member suggested I try a different day. Now I'm an integral part of the Thursday morning shift. It's the best! Everyone is trashy and loose. We go to movies together. One of the group often climbs up on a packing crate and sings Supremes songs or show tunes to the delight of the rest of us. He can really sing! I like to go out dancing with him. This same hunky young man cycled in the DC-Philly AIDS bike ride. Everyone in our shift chipped in and sponsored him. I made him a T-shirt saying, 'I'm riding for MANNA.' Thinking about us apparently helped him get up some of the grueling hills.

"There's another member of my group, a retired elementary school teacher, I describe as the chief fascist. She's the 'portion control queen,' and nobody challenges her. She knows her stuff and is a great person. Another man keeps the group interested with his talk of 'toxic shame' and vitamin supplements. Two helpful, smart, and eager high school students from Friends Select and two retired school nurses are also part of our crew.

"Working at MANNA is my favorite thing to do every week, even though the work is mundane. I scrub dishes, fetch things up, in fact, whatever the chefs ask. But the people are fabulous. When I changed jobs, I protected my Thursday mornings. I wouldn't accept a new job if I couldn't stick with my Thursday crowd.

"My family is supportive of my work with MANNA. My eight- and ten-year-olds have both been to MANNA. They know about AIDS. We don't shield them. AIDS is part of life, part of what is horrible and wrenching. When they're a little older, I'll get them more involved, but this past Halloween they helped me make trick-or-treat bags for the kids who receive MANNA meals. I raised $60 in donations from people at work. My children decorated and stuffed the bags with candy, stickers, rings, and spiders, and they were sent to the MANNA children. It made our Halloween extra special.

"Over the eighteen months I've volunteered, I've seen an increase in the volume of food prepared and a number of changes. Recently there was some 'bureaucratic nonsense,' but it settled down quickly. For example, I was recently banned from using MANNA's public address system. Most people just say, 'Food on the dumb waiter,' but I'm flamboyant and I got carried away. They asked me to stop because it distracted too many people. I accepted this. I trust others to make the decisions because I can't stand being on committees. I'm a front-line person. I just work in the kitchen.

"Volunteering on Thursday mornings is about 75 percent sheer enjoyment. However, we never forget what we are doing, making meals which are going to someone else's best friend. I think I'll be volunteering at MANNA for a long time."

Fulfillment in Menial Work

We have received many messages from our volunteers that are both sobering and poignant. One day I got a letter from Major Fenwick telling me what it was like to work at MANNA. He was seventy-seven and retired. In the 1960s, after leaving the Marine Corps, the major had owned a restaurant and did all the cooking. He always wanted to use his culinary skills again. That's what drew him to MANNA. However, he worked the afternoon shift and spent all his time chopping vegetables. He was saying he got little satisfaction from this task because it was tedious and boring. He was envious of the morning crew because they got to cook. I was about to call our volunteer coordinator to see if the major could be transferred into a morning shift where he'd be given the opportunity to cook. However, I paused because the letter seemed to be veering into something needing closer attention. "I've devoted two years of my life to chopping carrots and onions," he wrote. "It's tedious. I dread these chores. They feel endless, like cutting off the ends of string beans for four hundred meals. I also hate peeling potatoes. By the way, there's not a decent peeler in the place. Can we buy some new peelers, or should I bring one from home?"

He went on to say that MANNA needed to use its volunteers better and give them a greater variety of tasks. He acknowledged how hard it was to make good use of all the talents the volunteers brought, but he exhorted MANNA to work harder at this. He highlighted that he loved it when everything went wrong at MANNA. These days were exciting because everyone had to improvise, and sometimes he even got to cook. He also pointed out several things we all knew, that we had inadequate space and the staff was stretched too thin. The tone of the major's letter was such that I wondered if there were things that needed rectifying at MANNA's core. I was surprised and delighted by what he said next.

"These things aside, volunteering at MANNA is satisfying. There's a phenomenon here, like the one I experienced when I was in the Marines. Because the same people work in the same shift, special relationships get formed and we develop an esprit de corps, the byproduct of group cohesiveness. Even our discontents bond us together. Also I feel I am the 'sociometric center,' by which I mean that somehow I feel everything revolves around me when I'm volunteering. I enjoy this feeling. Others are always acknowledging me as a special person, and that makes me feel important. When I arrive, they say things like, 'Everything is under control now that the major is here!' It's funny. They say that stuff to everyone, but it always touches me anyway. It makes me laugh, and I feel part of something special. In my shift there is a group of five who are my age. We talk about issues and experiences that affect us. They are a good age group for me to work with. There are also many wonderful young people. They are fun to be around."

I was temporarily distracted by a phone call and then I got involved in other tasks. Before I knew it the day was done. I threw the major's letter in my briefcase and read it later that night after the children were in bed. I was delighted by the other side of MANNA he showed me that evening.

"MANNA is clear that you want people involved in every aspect of meal preparation. Instead of using sophisticated food chopping machines, we do without such equipment. If we used such machines there would be no need for people like me to cut vegetables. I know what you're up to! Mechanization takes away from human interaction in doing mundane chores, but it is the human interaction that is the most important. What makes this food special is that we work so hard and put so much of ourselves into these meals. It is prepared with love. We do figure out how to work together, and the food is special because of what we have put into it. And even with the most mundane chores, we manage to make them meaningful for us.

"When I see a problem I don't speak up. I have opinions about how things should be done, but I keep quiet and do what I'm asked. I appreciate MANNA's purpose and choose to be dutiful, but not compliant. If I see a better way to chop onions, I show by example, rather than telling everyone what I think they should do.

"It's important for me to learn how to be a good follower. Learning to submit to other people's guidance even when you're not sure it's the best way is all part of the growing I'm still doing. When I and everyone else do our assigned duties, the meals get made and people with AIDS get to eat great food, lovingly prepared. It is important for me to respect what the staff asks of me. Being and becoming a good follower was not why I volunteered for MANNA, but that's what it's become for me.

"Doing good works is the underpinning of the Jewish religion. That's what MANNA is for me. It gives me the chance to do good deeds for others. It's a way for me to live out our faith.

"What's been special about my time at MANNA is I've been finding the work meaningful even though the actual jobs are boring. Someone once said, 'It's not the events of your life that matter; it's what you do with those events.' At MANNA it's not *what* you do that matters, it's that *you do it with love.*"

The letter was signed, "Yours Sincerely, Major C. J. Fenwick."

I spent the rest of that evening reading this letter over and over, until it's message sunk into crevices not normally accessible to me. "It's not what you do that matters; it's that you do it with love." That proved to be the essence of MANNA.

Laura's Psalm

In my view one of MANNA's greatest vulnerabilities could easily slide under the table and be out of our awareness for so long that we became accustomed to not even thinking about it. The concern was two-pronged. One side was that the food MANNA prepared and delivered, which was originally understood as a tangible expression of the community's caring, might become an actual substitute for the love it was intended to express. We knew that "the food has to be prepared with love, it has to be delivered with love, and the funders have to provide their resources with love." Were it not for that love, MANNA's food might fill one's stomach for a few hours just like a hamburger from a fast food joint, but it could not be a means of sustaining the soul. The other prong was that the quality of MANNA's loving might become smothering, syrupy, disempowering, or self-serving.

One tension we lived with perpetually was how much to do for those we were serving. We wanted to offer people what they genuinely needed but not to create false dependencies. The resources we were drawing upon belonged to the community at large and we had to be good stewards. We debated constantly who should be the recipient's of MANNA's services. Should we serve only the homebound? What was a valid definition of "homebound?" Should we prepare meals for large groups and serve them in a church hall? Should we open MANNA TAKEOUT? Strong voices emerged on every side of this issue. Some thought MANNA's meals should be only for those who had no other way to care for themselves. Others thought we should get involved in countering the wasting syndrome earlier and that we should increase the nutritional quality of the food eaten by all people living with HIV before the debilitating symptoms of AIDS set in.

These debates were healthy, because the issues were out in the open, and whenever we got mired in the everydayness of what MANNA was doing, someone like Laura spoke up to keep us focused:

"For me delivering food to shut-ins with AIDS is not just a job. It is a journey to healing. Every mile I drive, every door I open, and every meal I serve helps me deal with losing my brother to AIDS. I've been doing this job with my husband every Friday for two years, and I am thankful for what it has opened me up to.

"I have seen much dying since I began with MANNA. The first was not AIDS related. One day I arrived and the lover of one of our regular clients had died of a freak accident. I stayed with this man to comfort him. MANNA didn't demand that I get back out on my route and make my next delivery. They trusted that I would make the right decision. They valued one client's welfare as much as anything else. Since then seven of the people I have delivered to have died. On two occasions the client had died the morning I was making a delivery. We stopped to help deal with the body and prepare for the morticians to arrive.

"MANNA is a special place. Most of us, the staff and the volunteers, have experienced a personal loss due to AIDS. As a result, we all have a vested interest in MANNA and its purpose. We use our pain to fuel our commitment to MANNA's mission.

"No matter what your function is in the organization, it will bring you closer to a inner resolution to whatever troubles you. If you cry while you're slicing the carrots, it's okay. It's part of the healing.

"I have the privilege of serving MANNA's meals to the needy, but that's just a part of it. I know the people on my route very well by now. Hence I can give comfort when family members are absent. I hold a hand when death comes close. I offer support to the one who has lost a lover. I feel much more than just a provider of food. I feel like a carrier of the community's love and concern. I always feel I'm on a mission. And by some process which is a mystery to me, that has been helping my own healing."

Curious Insight

At MANNA we often longed for wisdom captured on tablets of stone. What we knew seemed like etchings in the sand, which could vanish with tomorrow's wind. It was hard running an organization where today's success could make tomorrow a failure, where more could be less and vice versa, where drawing a boundary to ensure a particular outcome might produce the opposite effect, where we had to rely on the very ones most likely to let us down.

We could easily conclude that if only our knowledge base was more adequate, or if we were a bit smarter, or a bit more something that we weren't, we wouldn't be caught in such conundrums. We craved to be rid of our feelings of vulnerability.

I'm sure the ancient wanderers in the desert knew something of the frustration we felt, despite the difference in our contexts. They were always living on a precarious edge. Even the manna that came today could be turned off tomorrow if God so deemed. And the Almighty was being pretty circumspect about the consequences for following or not following His commands. History tells us that the Israelites received manna every day for forty years. However, as they lived each day, they did not really know if tomorrow's supply would actually show up, or if this promise of daily bread was forever. It had to be a struggle for them to be so dependent on this handout, with all its curious quirks. No wonder they were eager to get to the land flowing with milk and honey, where they wouldn't have to be so reliant on such a hard-to-satisfy God. We also know, thanks to the benefit of hindsight, that this generation of Israelites, to whom the Ten Commandments had been given and who were being molded into the Jewish people, were not the ones who were ultimately going to inhabit the promised land. It was the offspring of these former slaves who were to enjoy the freedoms for which they had labored so long.

One could understand if they complained to Moses. "Okay, so you say God is preparing us. And that requires us passing some tests. But we're tired of these hoops we're having to jump through. Where is it getting us? We're still locked out here in the desert."

The ancient texts indicate that Moses ultimately got fed up with their complaining and that God became perturbed by their fickleness, but at least in the pre-manna days, their griping was treated as an acknowledgment of their vulnerability. And the Lord's initial response was not to rebuke them or dismiss them as weaklings, but to invite them to draw near, for their vulnerability was the soil in which could be planted lessons for the ages.

Every gardener knows that for a seed to grow and bear fruit it must be placed in fertile soil, watered faithfully, and warmed by the sun. The same is true for spiritual growth. MANNA taught us that authentic acknowledgment of our vulnerability takes away the spirit's barrenness, that the tears of the aching heart are the soul's watering can, and the refining fires of our existence provide sunshine for the inner being. I once railed against this, lamenting that God had not devised a better redemptive system. Today I marvel at how fruitful the spirit is when our individual and collective vulnerability is felt with all its raging force. In experiencing this at MANNA we tapped into a source of strength that had previously been foreign to most of us.

Were it not for our hunger, there would never had been any manna. Had it not been for our thirst, we might never have known about the waters of life. Were it not for our vulnerability we might never have accessed the strength latent in the collective spirit.

Frankly, I'm delighted those chosen to bring the awareness of God's presence into our everyday life were spiritually underdeveloped. They seemed more like me and the people I know. That helped me identify with their learning. Had God selected some spiritual giants to make the discovery that we are all children of God, beloved and cared for every moment of every day, would this realization have been as meaningful to the rest of us?

Through all of history, the Almighty has chosen many individuals who knew a lot about vulnerability to broadcast the divine news to the people. Moses, as an infant, was plucked from those slated to be killed. David, the great king, started as a lad with a slingshot and a few stones when he set out to do battle with Goliath. Job had to descend into deep despair before he was spiritually accessible to God. Amos was a mere shepherd, an alien and an outcast, when he called for "justice to roll down like waters and righteousness like an ever-flowing stream!" (Amos 5:24). John was clothed in the skin of a beast and eating wild locusts when his voice crying in the wilderness pointed to "the way of the Lord." Siddhartha was a runaway prince when he stumbled on, or was drawn into, enlightenment. Mohammed was an illiterate when he received the revelation that was to set a new spiritual course for so many. Martin Luther was a disillusioned member of the establishment when he tacked a few scraps of paper to a door and started a reformation.

Five

GIVING IS CONTAGIOUS

Lesson 5:
Love grew when given away.

T O PROVIDE A TANGIBLE REMINDER of God's faithfulness
to future generations Moses was instructed to store a
small portion of the manna in a jar and place it before the
Holy Ark. Henceforth manna would be seen as both the
food that saved the children of Israel from starvation and
the symbol of God's healing grace given them at the nadir
of their brokenness. The message, to be recalled forever, was
that their vulnerability was fully matched by God's generosity,
that "the life-threatening scarcity of the wilderness could be
transformed into a place of wondrous abundance."[10]

The science behind the miracle of manna and the psychological mechanism by which the soul's scarcity was converted
into a source of spiritual abundance was never explained.
However, the Scriptures tell us that the children of Israel kept
manna, and the jar with a residue of the bread from heaven,
at the center of their faith.[11]

Since that first long journey through the wilderness bread
has been the food that sustains the body and also the symbol
that all are cherished by God. A sweet reminder of this lesson
came during World War II. Many orphaned children, rescued
from starvation and afraid of what the next day might bring,
were unable to sleep. Then someone suggested they each be
given a piece of bread to hold at bedtime. This comforted

the traumatized youngsters and enabled them to fall asleep. A simple piece of bread brought the miracle of rest to kids ravaged by the obscenities of war.[12]

Manna had several peculiarities. Those who collected a lot, had the same quantity when it was measured as those who had picked up little. Then no matter how much they ate all were satisfied to the same degree. This is a logical absurdity: it says in essence that if you overeat or merely nibble all are nourished to the same extent. The Talmud also says that the manna did not have to be cooked, spiced, sauced, or prepared in any special way, because it arrived with "the flavor of every conceivable dish."[13] One only had to desire a certain meal and that was how the manna tasted. This was the kind of culinary trick one might find at the Monty Python Restaurant: each patron makes a selection from a long menu with great variety but is served the same generic meal. All leave fully satisfied, however, because the special flavors, dormant in the food, were released by the minds of the consumers.

The gift of food at times of sadness and mourning is a custom passed down through the ages. A special meal cooked on one's own stove or a loaf of homemade bread has often served as an eloquent way to express caring to a friend overwhelmed by grief, illness, or despair. The time spent in the kitchen also nourishes the giver. The act of holding the aching one in the heart seems to help one sense God's presence in the rising yeast, in the enriching aromas, in the chemical reactions by which grain becomes bread.

The sacred writings state repeatedly that when we take our brokenness, let ourselves feel blessed for the bit of our essence we can access, and then give our fragmented selves away, we are transformed. No story illustrates this more profoundly than what happened to Glen, a member of the MANNA inner circle from Germantown Methodist Church.

Bathed in Sunlight

"Soon after MANNA began a beloved member of our church died," reported Glen. "Although Richard had a tight circle of friends in our congregation, many did not even know he was gay, let alone that he had AIDS and was soon to be snatched from our midst. I had known him for years. Caring for Richard taught us that MANNA was less about what we were doing for others and more about becoming open to the unknown parts of ourselves. John Donne's exhortation — 'Never ask for whom the bell tolls, it tolls for thee' — was a message for us."

Two decades earlier, Richard had been drafted to fight in Vietnam. Forced to become an adult by the atrocities of war, he coped with the death of others before their time by looking after a few children orphaned by random bombs dropping from the sky. By midlife he was a victim of the biological bomb exploding at random in our own backyard and was like the needy child requiring daily tending. He had once tried to cure his own aching heart by caring for the needy. It had become his turn to offer a balm to our aching hearts by being the gracious recipient of our care.

Glen longed to be touched by a transcendent loving, but he never expected that waiting upon Richard as he waited for his passage to the other side would alter his heart so profoundly. Although at the time he could not discern God's Quiet Presence in the tumult of Richard's illness, he later recognized the transformation begun in him as his buddy was taken away.

The day Richard was to die he called Glen at work. Knowing the end was near, Glen dropped everything, jumped in his car, and raced over. Richard was very agitated. He wanted something, but nothing Glen did offered any comfort. After a while Glen did the only thing he could think of. Without even taking off his jacket or his shoes, he climbed onto Richard's bed and held his withering body as it slipped in and out of consciousness. In life Glen had never held his friend in a long embrace, yet in death it felt right and simple. At what seemed like a random moment, Glen gently kissed him and whispered, "Richard, I love you." With that simple gesture, the room became awash with calm and the beads of perspiration that had been forming on Richard's lips and brow were released, and like a gentle stream the passage from this world to the next occurred.

"Richard's death changed me. It all began that day," Glen said. "That was nine years ago but I can still recall the details of his last hours. When I close my eyes I can see the translucent light in the sweat drenching his face. With Richard's passing, death became real to me. Other people I loved had died, my dad, my grandfather, but this was different. From that moment on everyone's life, mine included, was more precious because henceforth death felt ever present."

Descent into Depression

After Richard died Glen took a break from MANNA. While he had been happy serving as one of Richard's caretakers, being in this role again stirred up a host of feelings he thought had long been buried. Soon Glen was feeling a level of depression he'd never experienced in his thirty-five years.

Glen had been forced to become a caretaker when he was still young. He was the oldest of four children and was eleven when his last sibling was born. By his mid-teens Glen had spent a lot of years looking after kids. While today Glen looks like he was made for this role, when he was a teenager it crushed him. It wasn't that he couldn't handle the tasks. The problem was there was no point when his family let his needs be put in the spotlight or moved to center stage. Glen was through adolescence before the young child in him even had a chance to breathe.

As an adult Glen felt paralyzing hostility toward his parents because the choices they made had unwittingly limited the options he had as a child. Not that he wanted his reality to change, for it was the only one he knew. He loved his brothers and sister and was proud that together they had made a life for themselves in their troubled family. Glen just wanted to have different feelings about his past. In particular he wanted to be free of the rage he felt toward his parents that had kept him captive for so long.

Glen felt his parents wanted to be seen as having a perfect family but refused to let any real emotions be expressed in their home. "I could not stand the falseness. I could not stand that they had no relationship with each other, let alone with us kids. I could not stand that they refused to communicate with each other. I could not stand that their constant message to us was that we kids were not okay," Glen reported. "On the outside we looked like the ideal family but on the inside we were all drowning. We only discussed the trivial while the important issues were trivialized. If we dared have a feeling about the twisted way we operated, that emotion was quickly silenced. Today when I see kids going through things like this I can't stand it. I want to rescue them. This, of course, is because I want to rescue myself from my own past."

Glen's father was a successful lawyer who provided well for their financial needs but was always absent, literally and figuratively. Even when home he was disengaged or became irrationally enraged when a child did something as human as spilling a glass of milk. Yet on Sunday, as they all were marched off to church, he took pride in the appearance of their wholesomeness, even though Glen's mother had been forced to abandon her strong Methodist roots to satisfy his father's investment in presenting a Catholic facade. Glen felt his mother was rendered ineffective by the demand to keep it all together and to ensure that the ever-present brittleness remained hidden. Of course, the energy poured into concealing the self-evident only increased the family's fragility and the negative impact it had on the children.

Glen first let his troubled past come into his awareness with all its force when his grandfather died unexpectedly. "I was nineteen. At the funeral I lost it. This was the guy who saved my soul, and he was gone. He was the one person who had taken me under his wing, showed me that I was loved, and let me know what being human was like. Often, when he saw what was going on in my family, I'd notice him keeping back a tear. He was the person who wept the tears I could not express. I don't know what would have become of me, had it not been for him. He loved to garden, and he grew wonderful roses. My favorite thing to do as a child was to climb into his hammock, which hung under a canopy of roses he had planted and carefully nurtured. Swinging together under the thorns and colorful petals, we talked about nothing in particular, but our conversations made me feel special. After his funeral I would not leave the cemetery. The next morning they came and found me. I was still sitting on the mound covering his body. I would not go home. What I needed most all those years was a simple connection with another human being. He was that for me. He loved me, cared for me, wept for me, and celebrated with me. I never got to thank him. I never got to tell him that he saved me.

"When I was twenty-eight my dad died. I didn't expect his death either. I never was reconciled with him about anything. He was so heavy-handed. Mom too. She'd also smack us, but at least with her you knew what you had done. With Dad he'd strike us for no obvious reason. Of course, he'd invent a justification, but it never felt real. Here's an example. When my parents went out, I was in charge. One night I let all the kids stay up later than usual. We were visiting a neighbor's house when we saw our parents coming back early. We all took off at high speed and scrambled into bed, trying not to get caught. My parents saw us. Imagine how funny it must have been to see those little charging feet racing across the lawn, desperate to get back undetected. Do you think my parents could make a special moment out of something like this? My dad beat us all and really scared us that night! Raw images like this kept swirling around in me for years. They would not go away.

"Then, of course, there was my homosexuality. This was so very troubling. Oh my God, what it is to grow up in a supposedly devout Catholic family and be gay! By the time I was in college I knew I was gay. How on earth was I ever going to embrace my homosexuality! I eventually did quite a bit of therapy. That softened some of the issues, but I still could not accept being gay. What troubled me most was that I would never be a parent. There was nothing I ever wanted more in life than to be a father. And here I was located in a body that ensured I would never be a dad. As I entered adulthood society was showing no signs of letting gay men adopt children. To the contrary. This was the HIV era when all gay men were seen to be at risk or already infected and hence could never be trusted with a child. Many of our friends were ill or dying and all our spare time was spent being their caretakers, while those seeking a sexual partner had to risk getting a killer virus. It puzzles me how anyone thinks men actively *choose* to be homosexual!"

These were the conflicts resurfacing in Glen during the two-year sabbatical he took from MANNA. However, during the months following Richard's death, Glen noticed a shift occurring in him. In the beginning, it was subtle, but it became huge. He stopped seeing people as frail anymore and began to notice their strengths. He had witnessed, firsthand, the courage it took to endure extreme illness and then to embrace death. That led him to wonder if his wounds, his brokenness, his frailty, might turn out to be his strength too. He could not put it into words, but he knew Richard's passing had removed

his fear of death, and with that gone he felt life pulsating
through him in new and heightened ways.

The Call to Serve

Glen was on the verge of appreciating this when MANNA's
distribution coordinator called. "Glen, I know you are still on
sabbatical from MANNA, but I'm hoping you might be ready
to get back in the saddle. I'm in a crunch and need help."

"What do you need?" Glen asked.

"We have this couple, Tamika and Grover. She has just
returned from the hospital. Both of them are sick and need
the kind of care I know you are experienced at offering. Any
chance you could take a meal to them today?"

Glen had not prepared himself to reenter the emotional
fray, but before he had formulated a reasoned response he
said, "Where do they live?

"In New Jersey, about a ten-minute drive from your office.
You could pick up the meal from our New Jersey distribution
center, which is only a few miles from where you work."

Glen felt reticent about starting again, but it was hard to
say no to MANNA. Before they'd hung up he said, "I'll help
today and see how it works out for me."

When Glen arrived, the door was unlocked. He knocked,
and Grover, with a weak voice, called for him to come in. The
first thing Glen saw was a three-year-old boy, lying on his bed
and playing with a toy truck. Glen had not expected a child
and had only brought meals for Grover and Tamika, who was
not at home. The little boy jumped up, ran into Glen's arms,
and gave him a bear hug.

"So who are you?" Glen asked the boy in his arms.

"Charles" he replied proudly, with a big smile.

"Hi, Charles. This must be your dad. Will you please
introduce us?"

Grover was a forty-six-year-old African American man who

had seen great sadness. Over the last seven years he had become a father twice and had lost his daughter, Serina, to AIDS. Both he and his wife, Tamika, had the virus. Tamika had been very ill for a long time and had been at death's door for months. Grover had been reasonably well until a year ago. He had managed to hold down a job and to care both for Serina and Tamika. In recent months, however, he had been as sick as Tamika, and everything was getting very hard for them, especially as Charles grew and needed more attention. Grover was terribly upset when he spoke about the prospect that he and Tamika might not be around for long. His biggest concern was about what would happen to Charles, the only member of the family who had managed to escape the virus. Grover often silently cried himself to sleep, thinking about his son's future with no parents.

Grover was happy they had managed to stay together as a family throughout all the turmoil, but that offered little consolation now that the end was in sight for Tamika and him. They had only a small apartment, which they had got a year before after spending a few weeks in a homeless shelter. They had used all their resources caring for Serina. Their case manager was able to access some special funds of the Catholic Church, and that, along with their government money, had helped them stabilize for a while. Grover believed he would outlive Tamika and wanted to be able to care for Charles as long as possible.

Grover had no family to call upon. He had spent his whole childhood going from one foster family to another, and formed no significant ties with any of them. Tamika had three siblings and a mother, but they lived in various distant parts of the country and had long ago indicated they wanted nothing to do with a family infected with AIDS. Hence they felt very much on their own. They had no energy to cultivate friends and felt reliant on their own resources to care for Charles and themselves as best they could.

The pathos of this situation he had walked into, the joyous character of this young boy, and the obvious neediness of this household immediately touched Glen. He called the MANNA office, described the situation he had found, and said he was willing to deliver meals again and specifically asked to have a route that included Grover, Charles, and Tamika.

Glen became a regular meal deliverer for the family. During each visit he reserved some special time to play with Charles. Tamika especially appreciated this since Grover was getting weaker and did not have the energy to match his son's boyish exuberance. Glen took Charles for walks in the park and occasionally took him back to his office. Glen did whatever he could to give both Tamika and Grover some respite and to offer Charles a few extra moments in the sun, a little while longer out in the larger world, or a chance to play with some other children. During this first year, whatever seemed right, Glen did it. He hated seeing Charles cooped up and wanted to help him and his parents to remain together as long as possible. He recognized how much they all needed each other.

Then Tamika went into rapid decline and died suddenly one night. Charles was not quite four. It was traumatic for a young boy to see a parent die, and Grover was determined not to have this repeated when his own time came.

Almost without realizing it Glen was dropping by more and more often just to be with Charles and to give Grover some extra assistance. Glen marveled at how determined Grover was to do the best he could for Charles. Even when he was very weak and seemed close to death, he channeled the little energy he had to care for his son. On his rare good day Glen would invite Grover and Charles to his home for a meal or organize a special event like a trip to the circus. Before long Glen had become a major part of their support network. Charles had an occasional weekend sleepover at Glen's home, and one summer he even joined Glen and a group of his friends for their annual vacation.

Glen included Charles in as many normal events in his life that he could: the Fourth of July picnic with friends from work, trick or treating in his local neighborhood, and so on. Charles had a contagious smile and was always happy to be with other children. However, Glen said, "you could see the sadness in his eyes. He would never speak of his mother or his sister, both of whom he had watched die. He had suffered so much loss, and his little heart must have ached something awful."

The level of involvement Glen developed with this family was unusual for a MANNA volunteer; we were opening new territory, and many special relationships were developing that went well beyond a meal at lunch time.

Grover finally recognized he could no longer provide adequately for his son. One day, with no warning, Grover phoned Glen from his hospital bed to say he had just signed over custody to the state, and Charles was about to be placed in foster care. He asked Glen to be present when the social worker arrived to take him away. Glen knew how hard this decision was for Grover and that it took courage to ask for gut-wrenching help like this.

Years later Glen still wept as he described that afternoon. "May 21, 1995, was one of the most painful days of my life. A social worker was to pick up Charles from the home of the hospital chaplain, who had befriended Grover during his recent stays in the hospital. When Charles was asked to get in the car, I begged to go with him to his new home, a couple of hours away in Summit, New Jersey. I wanted to be sure that he would be safe, physically and emotionally, in his new surroundings. Of course, the answer was a firm no. My promise to Charles at that parting and all other partings since was that I would see him again soon."

Maintaining relationships became much more complicated. The first parental visit was scheduled for ten days later in Summit. Grover had recently been released from the hospital and was still very weak. There was no way he could make it on his own, so Glen offered to take him. Grover needed a lot of care.

The scene at the agency where the parental visits occurred was complex. Charles's foster parents were very kind and managed their part of the arrangement well. However, Glen and Grover were able to visit Charles only in the space supervised by the social worker. They could not go out anywhere. Since Glen was an unknown figure, the social worker sat nearby and diligently watched all his interactions with Charles. There were also many other parents and children in the room, and chaos ruled. Grover was extremely ill and had limited ability to cope. It was left to Glen to make the visit memorable for Charles. He had some books, so the two of them spent most of the time on the floor reading together.

This visit was the first of many over the next few months. Every other Friday Glen took time off work and visited with Charles, taking Grover along when he was well enough. Glen was always in the position of trying to make something meaningful out of nothing. "One winter day I arrived with a plastic bag full of snow. I put the plastic on the floor and with Charles made a snow man right there in the room. I had collected some stones and brought a carrot with me. What a mess — which we then had to clean up!

"At the time I didn't ask why I was putting so much effort into remaining connected to Charles," Glen said. "It just seemed the right thing to do. People said to me, 'You're crazy to jeopardize a good job by spending so much time on one kid!' I know it seemed strange, but something special was happening to me. As a result of my bonding with this child I was learning how to reconnect to the child in me. I had never been read to as a child, so I dealt with that by making sure Charles was read to. I had no connection with anyone except my grandfather, so I made sure this boy had an emotional tie to someone. I had never felt loved, so I let Charles know he was loved. As I did these things, my own heart became fuller, and with a fuller heart, my own pain faded into insignificance beside the struggles Grover and his son were going through."

Grover died in September 1995. Glen was present. He was driving past on his way back to the office. Since he had not seen Grover for a couple of days, Glen decided to drop in. When he arrived, a houseguest, an acquaintance in need of a bed, yelled to Glen that Grover was having difficulty breathing. They called the paramedics. The houseguest, apparently terrified of death, was screaming. Glen tried to calm her down so he could be with Grover, who had choked, and was unconscious. His breathing was faint and sporadic. Glen sat and held his hand until he took his last breath. Two days earlier Glen, realizing Glover was in desperate need of fluids, had tried to get him to the hospital, but Grover had refused. He was already too close to death to start backing away.

Glen told the paramedics how to contact Tamika's mother, Charles's grandmother, the closest living relative, and Grover's body was taken to the morgue. Glen suggested it might be nice for Charles if his dad were to be buried beside his mother and his sister. The few relatives available all agreed, but they were all keeping their distance. However, no one could recall where the others had been laid to rest. Some thought their ashes had been placed under a tree, but no one knew which tree. Glen decided to find out. He had the dates of death and asked the officials at the morgue what records they had. The reply was that the ashes were still at the morgue. They had been waiting for someone to collect them. Glen proposed to the family that both parents and Serina be buried in a cemetery on the outskirts of Baltimore, near where Tamika and Grover had grown up. All agreed. So on a beautiful afternoon Glen went to the morgue and picked up all the ashes of Charles's family. He felt honored to take the remains of these dear souls away from a dank building to a place where Charles could start the process of appropriating his heritage.

The burial was simple. Together Charles, Glen, and Tamika's mother dug a hole, mixed the ashes together, and placed them in the earth. Glen was meeting Charles's grandmother for the first time and was glad for her clear acceptance of her grandson. But he was disturbed that she insisted that the grave be left unmarked, for reasons Glen could not grasp. Glen bit his lip, silently vowing to give Charles the option of placing names on the grave after Tamika's mother died. She was already in her mid-seventies and Glen figured that by the time Charles was an adult he would be free to make his own choices. Glen also asked if he could take a few of the ashes in a zip-lock bag so that when Charles was a little older and understood more of the significance of his parent's lives, he could have a little burial ceremony of his own. Tamika's mother said "fine."

For the next few years Glen faithfully took Charles each spring to visit his grandmother. She lived a few miles from the cemetery in Baltimore, so they went to the grave at the same time, usually on a day of special remembrance, such as Tamika's birthday.

Life assumed some normalcy for a while. Charles lived with the same foster family in Summit, New Jersey, and Glen visited at least once a month. He also included Charles in special events such as vacations. At some point he became a respite caregiver. When the foster parents needed a break, Charles stayed for a while with Glen in his Germantown home. After a couple of years Glen took a new position with a law firm just north of Princeton and bought a home nearby. This made visiting easier because Charles lived only an hour away.

Then a crisis led Charles and the three other foster children staying with the Summit family to be transferred to new homes. Charles was separated from the other three foster children, which upset him greatly because they were beginning to feel like brothers and sister. The Department of Human Services was upset about this also and felt it was time to start looking for a permanent home for Charles. They had always anticipated that Charles's grandmother or Tamika's sister would adopt him when he got a little older, but this was not to be. So they made it known that in the next couple of years they would be looking for someone to adopt this fine, energetic, bright African American boy. Glen was both pleased and anxious. He was happy that Charles would no longer be shunted from foster home to foster home like his dad, Grover. But Glen was afraid the adopting family might not let the special relationship between him and Charles continue.

Daring to Dream

"Then from the cosmos came a thought I had never dared to consider," reported Glen. "The foster family caring for Charles asked if I would consider adopting him. "I said no! Actually I thought they were planning to adopt him. I was apparently wrong. What troubled me though was that I didn't even think I was an appropriate person to become the adoptive father! Imagine it. Of course I was the obvious person. I loved Charles. I was the one individual with a strong, continuous connection with him. There was just this one enormous problem. I was gay. And in our neck of the woods, they don't let gay men become dads. The thought tickled me though because my relationship with Charles was helping me to heal. Being with him through all his ups and downs had stopped me from wallowing in my own past. This boy embraced his pain with such honesty he was showing me what it meant to be connected to one's emotions. Caring for him was satisfying the part of me that always wanted to be a dad. He was giving me things I did not know I needed until I received them."

Everyone who witnessed the bond between Charles and Glen felt a more appropriate adoption would never be found, and the wheels started turning. While there was no guarantee the courts would go along with the plan, numerous social workers and adoption advocates began to mobilize so that Glen could become Charles' father.

Glen decided to pull out all the stops and see if the judicial system would approve the adoption. First he sought to become Charles's foster parent. That was approved. Then he had to enter the judicial process. In his adoption application Glen held nothing back. This was the right decision, for it was the quality of his heart that made him the father of choice. Glen laid out his own history, the journey he had walked, and how he and Charles had entered each other's lives. Then he addressed his feelings about Charles. This was what he wrote:

"On a recent weekend stay at my home, Charles completed his homework on his own at his desk in his second-floor bedroom. He asked me to take a look at it while he took his bath. He has good math abilities, and I found no mistakes that he had not already corrected. He has always enjoyed words and reading. One exercise asked that he use and underline vocabulary words in sentences. There in the middle of the page was a pair of sentences that spoke to me with a poignant message:

'The world is my *home*.'
'Glen, my toy *broke*.'

"Charles started life in suburban New Jersey with a bedridden mother and father, sometimes homeless, sometimes trapped in the worst part of a small city decimated by poverty; where he might be too close for my comfort to the scary and dangerous side of street life; where his father would cuddle him and sing "Old McDonald Had a Farm" and Charles would delight in adding his own special animals to that farm and we would all laugh at his tiger sounds; where he learned to spell 'red' and 'green' as we sat in my convertible at the intersection waiting for the lights to change on our way to and from his day care center, my house, or his dad's place; where he and I would share an apple on our way to the park and eventually at regular visits when he was a foster child in

Summit, sometimes driving in the country, where he met his first dairy cows grazing in the pasture and tickled me when he added a cow to our "Old McDonald's farm." Truly the world is his home.

"I like to imagine that, of all of the changeable faces in his world, I am one consistent and unconditional person in his life. I am there to remember all of the fun and the sadness of his life, even the names of those changeable faces who mattered so much to him. Like his teacher, Suzie, from the day care center; Charles asked if I remembered that she was the one who would fasten his overall straps when he got to day care because his dad wasn't able to do it at home. Charles asked me if I remembered when the kids at his day care blamed him for knocking over the play desk and teacher Suzie and I both assured him that he wasn't "bad." Like the time he asked me if I remembered his first foster parents and the day they all cried when his social worker came to tell him he had to leave and to say goodbye to his foster brothers and sister. Like the time Charles held his hand up to me and told me that he was getting whiter. When he repeated that phrase, I could only tell him with a smile on my face and holding my hand next to his, that this was his "winter color." In summer, the sun turns his skin a most glorious shade of brown. Like the time Charles told me how sad he was when he learned his father had died and wondered if I had told him of his death. He went on to ask me how I learned of his dad's death. With tears filling my own eyes, I told him I was there with his dad at the end. Who knows what it means, but I only hope that he is comforted to know that I'll be there to do my best when things seem out of his control and to remind him that the best we can do is to all lovingly work to try to understand each other.

"Knowing that children had never been part of the plan for my life made my decision to pursue this adoption very difficult. I had some low points when I thought I couldn't possibly manage it, especially alone. But I am working to understand what is important to me. My fears and joys are human, but I must be open to the full range of my emotions, and I know that I smile every time I think of Charles filling my home with the joyous sounds of his life. He will add so much to my sense of home and family, and I believe I will do the same for him. More than the food on the table, the faces (that have come and gone), the feelings that have touched each of us around that table, life is about nourishment for our bodies and our souls."

When the process got to the courts Glen was advised not to talk about being gay. Silence was the recommended path. Glen had to smile because this was how his family had chosen to deal with emotions too hard to handle in the light of day. But he went along with the script his advocates recommended. He hid nothing but only answered the questions formally asked of him. Everyone in the system knew this was going to be a gay adoption and frankly everyone privately approved. And so on a glorious day in 1999 Charles got a new family and Glen became a dad.

There was one person present at the formal adoption ceremony deserving of special mention, Glen's mother. "This is what happened to our relationship that day," said Glen. "Becoming a father changed my mother and my relationship with her forever. Despite the racism and homophobia, which had been rampant in my family, my mom claimed Charles as her special grandson that sunny afternoon and in so doing publicly declared her acceptance of me as a father and as a gay man. What a special gift. The inner shifts I had made were important too. I no longer saw my mother's attitudes, affect, or demeanor as a statement about me but merely as a reflection of who she was as a person with her own vulnerabilities, weaknesses, and frailties. But just as with Grover, Tamika and myself, I recognized these could also be her strengths. If I elected to treat them this way, all that had troubled me about my mother for so long might alter. I decided that henceforth I would cease to see her as limited or as anything for that matter, but would accept her for who she was." Glen had learned that when the child comes to love the parents for what they are, that actually frees the parent to move on to some new emotional places. This was one of the transformations Charles catalyzed in Glen's emotional development.

A puzzling question we at MANNA often asked ourselves was what led us to act as we did. In this case we asked, "what sparked the almost magical connection which began that day Charles first leapt into Glen's arms, continued to grow, and ultimately led to one of MANNA's first AIDS orphans helping to make gay adoptions possible in this region?" No answer to this could be adequate, but anyone who visits the home of Glen and Charles can palpably feel the love that binds them to each other.

One final image brings the story full circle and leaves joy in places not usually visited by laughter. "Soon after I bought my home just north of Princeton I decided to plant some roses," said Glen. "Rewind. My love of gardening is kindled by my grandfather, who helps me plant, prune, and grow all sorts of things around our home during my teens. We move some old rose bushes to a new spot beside the driveway. Alas, my dad arrives home with a new car, and the virgin thorns from our reborn roses scratch the side of his pride and joy. My angered father seizes an axe and cuts them down. Fast forward. Before I even have a garden in my new yard, with limited carpentry skill, I construct a trellis, a grand replica of the one my grandfather built decades ago. But I have no roses. So in the dark of night, I visit the old home, down in Washington, D.C., sold and resold to strangers, sneak in, and steal some clippings from my grandfather's rose plants. I plant them in my yard. They grow and blossom so gloriously they become the talk of the neighborhood. Pause. I become a new dad and Charles is trying to place his stamp on our home. 'Glen,' he says, 'we've got to get a hammock.' 'Great idea,' I reply. We head to the store and return with the best we can find. 'Where will we hang it?' I ask. 'I think it should go under the rose trellis,' Charles replies. 'Then we can lie on it together and look up at the beautiful flowers.' My heart privately misses a few beats. He has never heard the story of my relationship with my grandfather. He does not know that I feel my soul was rescued by my grandfather as we swung together in the hammock under his rose bushes.

"As Charles and I swing in our new hammock memories of my grandfather wash over me. Then I privately wonder when I will tell my son that in a fit of joy, I once took a pinch of his family's ashes, still sitting in the zip-lock bag waiting to be buried by him someday, and placed them near the roots of our rose bushes, a reincarnated version of the ones my grandfather had brought to life decades earlier. And as I look into his lively and engaging deep brown eyes, I thank God for the wisdom of MANNA's distribution coordinator who plucked me from my despondency and asked me to make a meal delivery to a needy family."

Six

IMPORTING PAIN

Lesson 6:
*MANNA became an importer of pain;
it had to learn how to manage pain internally
and not become an exporter of blame.*

WHILE THERE WERE MANY POSITIVE THINGS happening at MANNA, we were also encountering some really dark times that stretched us to the breaking point. In this chapter I discuss two events that exposed MANNA's underbelly: the dismissal of two staff upon whom we were completely reliant, and an ugly public fight we had with another Philadelphia AIDS organization that had helped nurture our growth. The dynamics initiated by these two organizational feuds, one internal and one external, set MANNA back substantially and flung MANNA forward precariously. We hated having to deal with these issues for they showed MANNA failing in the very domains we most aspired to succeed in. This led us to question if we had the skills to run this organization we hoped to create. Yet the refinements they brought to MANNA's functioning were far-reaching.

Dismissing Staff

First a little context. After a few years everyone noted that MANNA's staff was a highly caring and supportive group. When staff members were asked if they had any conflicts,

they replied, "All the time! But our conflicts are about how to
handle a rough situation, or because one of us got swamped
and let something drop. We get angry at each other, argue
about how to recover, reassign some priorities, and get on
with preparing that day's meals. We don't stay mad with each
other. We're all stressed to the limits, and the last thing we
need is to let things fester. We get the conflict out, let it
go, and move on." However, this collaborative spirit did not
always exist.

For its first years MANNA operated out of First Presbyterian Church, had access to the church kitchen only until
1:00 p.m., and used a converted Sunday School room as an
office. We were so cramped it was hard to be competent, especially as the demand for MANNA's services and the number
of volunteers grew.

The daily tasks of getting meals out were divided between
two functions: operations and kitchen. An operations manager fielded all requests for meals, contacted case managers
or physicians, recruited volunteers, assigned them to either
kitchen or meal delivery duty, tallied the number of meals
needed for the next day, and passed this on to the chef by late
afternoon. The chef created the menu, bought the produce
and, working with kitchen volunteers, prepared the meals,
placed them in containers, and got them ready for the volunteer deliverers to pick up at noon. Meanwhile the operations
manager created routes for the deliverers and had everything
ready to go when they arrived at lunchtime. Each task was
straightforward enough but the level of precision and timing
of the various tasks made every day complex.

MANNA was committed to being volunteer-based, and the
role of the staff was to support and guide the volunteer efforts.
While the manager and the chef had to ensure that everyone
in need of food was fed each day, they had to structure the
work so it was done by the volunteers. Staff were not to do the
work themselves, unless something fell between the cracks, in

which case they were to move into high gear and correct the problem, in a seamless way so that all volunteers experienced themselves as being successful. For MANNA to run effectively, a high level of coordination between the operations and kitchen functions was required. The two occupants of these positions had to maintain a strong, flexible, and collaborative working relationship.

The volume of work assigned to these two individuals was too much. We all knew this, but at the time MANNA had no resources to hire more staff. The only way to expand our services was to invent new ways for the volunteers to do more of the key tasks, but the only people able to do this redesign work were the manager and the chef, whose energies were already overtaxed.

Soon the relationship between the chef and the manager was at the breaking point. The tensions they experienced were organizational in nature, but they both personalized them. Each started blaming the other for anything that went wrong, and day after day MANNA's executive director, Gwendolyn, was drawn from her primary tasks of institution building and garnering funds to deal with the fast-degenerating chef-manager relationship. What made it difficult was that both these staff members, against all odds, were doing an excellent job, volunteers were being shielded from their strife, and MANNA's reputation in the community was growing weekly.

Gwendolyn made many attempts to mediate their relationship, but the two combatants saw her as part of the problem. Gwendolyn sought my help, arguing that more staff had to be recruited. But we were not able to find quick money to pay any more people, and it would be months before we heard from foundations to which we had sent proposals seeking funds for new staff. I then inserted myself into the middle of these relationships. That made things worse. As board chair, I had not developed the board fast enough to generate the dollars needed and hence was a fair target for their blame, which rendered my interventions ineffective.

One conversation between the chef and the manager, which occurred in my presence, captured the essence of their conflict. The chef, fuming at the manager, said, "At 4:00 p.m. yesterday you told me we needed forty-seven meals today. So last night I went to the market when they dramatically reduce prices. I bought salmon for forty-seven." The chef was always working to minimize costs and prepared the next day's menu based on what produce could be purchased at the last minute for a good price. The capacity of our chef to create nutritious meals at low cost was a skill I valued greatly.

Speaking directly to the manager the chef continued. "Then this morning you told me to prepare fifty-one meals, not forty-seven. That threw my planning off. I had to do some last-minute adjustments and go to the supermarket again myself. Then when we were fifteen minutes late with the meals today you got angry with me!"

"I'm sorry," the manager responded, "but overnight several of our clients were released from the hospital and called saying they needed meals today. We've got to be more flexible. Our job is to accommodate all who call. It is my responsibility to ensure that MANNA delivers on its promise." The manager once more repeated the position stated many times before. "Don't cut things so tight. If the number is forty-seven buy a few extra steaks, even if we waste a little money. Then we can accommodate last-minute changes and we won't. . . . "

"It's not that simple," the chef interjected. "Given the limited capacity of our oven we can't cook more than forty-eight salmon steaks at a time. This requires scheduling the work differently. Until we get the new stoves we've been promised for weeks and some more volunteers. . . . " The chef fell silent and looked at me in exasperation.

Things had been extra hard that day. Two kitchen volunteers did not show up, and one deliverer had called in sick. Both the manager and Gwendolyn had ended up making several meal deliveries. The stoves had been delayed again because they could not be installed until new exhaust vents were built. We were forever whiplashed by unpredictable schedules of workers and licensing inspectors.

Neither Gwendolyn nor I could come up with any quick fixes and were just as responsible for this dilemma as the manager and the chef. The executive director tried to siphon off some of the blaming dynamic they were caught in. This worked for a while, but the relationship between the chef and the manager got caught in squeeze after squeeze, and the acrimony between them grew. Gwendolyn was near the end of her rope. Meanwhile the positions of the chef and the manager became more rigid. Eventually, at one of their meetings "to clear the air" each presented Gwendolyn with an ultimatum: "Either the chef leaves or I do," said the manager. "The manager leaves or I do," stated the chef. While this organizational problem had to be dealt with by organizational means, we were out of time. This conflict had grown so personalized it had become a showdown about who was the real villain.

There seemed no alternative than to accept that either or both would leave. To lose both these staff members at the same time would present serious problems because the knowledge each had acquired was yet to be institutionalized and would vanish with their departures. However, that seemed a better option than to continue in the same vein. Gwendolyn sought the board's counsel.

A small group of us met and decided to ask the manager to leave. We felt we could not delay revamping this job, and since the tasks performed by the operations manager would be in flux for a while, we thought it was the thing to work on first. The manager was very upset and claimed that the chef was equally responsible, a view we shared. However, we decided to address one issue at a time.

We felt bad. The operations manager had served MANNA well, and to be forced out under a cloud made it hard for this person to be given the much-deserved public recognition.

Without knowing where the funds would come from, we created two positions to replace the operations manager: a volunteer coordinator and a distribution coordinator. For a while everything was calm. However, the growth in the number of people needing meals was relentless, and within another year MANNA hit the limit of what could be produced in the church. We had to relocate, but things did not move fast enough for the chef, who tried to dramatize the plight by refusing to prepare all the meals needed one day, arguing it was unjust to be told to keep expanding the amount of food to be produced without ever providing any extra resources. The pressures being placed on the kitchen crews were unreasonable, but this unilateral action effectively forced MANNA to operate a wait list, which was against board policy. We delivered to everyone who needed food, even if it meant we had to purchase meals from restaurants.

Leadership's response indicted that we too had grown rigid. We refused to have a wait list because it was counter to our goals. We were unwilling to accept any sense of failure, real or imagined, or to hold back services so political pressure for more funds would build. The reality was we expected too much of our staff. Acting out our own inflexibility, we labeled the chef's actions as unacceptable. Some board members wanted the chef to be dismissed. However, Gwendolyn, embodying our flexible side, was not convinced. She was more forgiving than most.

The chef's provocation sped up the move to a new facility but also left some shadowy consequences. The complaints coming from the kitchen grew more vociferous and more acrimonious, and in Gwendolyn's view minor aggravations were being blown out of proportion. She recognized that the chef had been filled with emotion, and the dams, which had long kept difficult feelings contained, were beginning to crack. Gwendolyn was the focus of all the animosity. She did not like this but tolerated it. However, the chef's emotions began spilling out everywhere and contaminating the kitchen crews, which were being slowly mobilized to join in a revolt against the executive director. When Gwendolyn discovered this, her tolerance expired. She announced forcefully, "It is time to pack your apron and leave." The chef warned that this dismissal would cause MANNA to fall apart. Gwendolyn acknowledged that many criticisms leveled at her were valid, that staff had never been given sufficient back up or adequate time off, but explained that this was why she'd given the chef the benefit of the doubt for so long.

The chef was stunned to be fired and told Gwendolyn to expect kitchen volunteers to leave in droves, but that never happened. While one part of the chef hoped the cooking crews would quit and bring MANNA to a halt, this was balanced by an equally strong wish that no one receiving MANNA meals ever be hurt. The chef departed quietly, albeit angrily. I am deeply grateful for all that this culinary maestro did for MANNA and the community.

This was a sad moment for all involved. However, years later, the story of this chef was coded into MANNA's folklore as follows: "This person made a great contribution but let self-interest get in the way of MANNA's service to people living with AIDS. Anyone whose ego gets too large or engages in power plays does not last long in this organization."

Once the dust kicked up by these losses had settled, we asked ourselves whether we had escalated our expectations of the chef and the operations manager beyond all possibility and then blamed them for being inadequate. Had they become sacrificial lambs? Our answer was yes. We were sad that, despite our efforts to have it play out some other way, we had been unsuccessful.

Fighting over Resources

As MANNA began we made a commitment to stay out of AIDS politics and to build collaborative relationships with other HIV agencies. We failed at both these goals before we were able to succeed. Partnering with those who had been "freedom fighters" from the earliest days was difficult, in part because we did not know, in our collective gut, the magnitude of the fight in which the HIV community as a whole had been forced to engage.

Also we were representatives of the church. That caused some to be justifiably cautious of us. In the 1980s numerous church people, even preachers, had stated publicly that gays deserved what they were getting, and that AIDS might be God's punishment. While this was not the position of First Presbyterian Church, it was easy to lump all churches together. Many who had been dedicated to the fight for gay rights and acceptance of AIDS as a public health crisis affecting everyone found the position of the church as a whole to be myopic, uninformed, and heartless. The seeming indifference of churches like ours, only a couple of years earlier, was what they had been fighting against. We had yet to put more than our toes into the AIDS waters. No one knew, not even us, whether MANNA would stay the course, especially when things got tough and politically messy.

Against this backdrop, did we have any right to expect that the established AIDS organizations in Philadelphia, especially those committed to political activism, should trust MANNA or applaud us for the small, white-glove, pristine contribution we planned to make? When we said we would keep out of AIDS politics, this could well have been interpreted as code for: "We will not get into the trenches; we will not risk leaving any of our blood on the battlefields." We were nevertheless going to be the beneficiaries of all the fighting they had been forced to do! Our "we will not fight" posture could easily have been interpreted as an indictment of all the battles others had started, fought, lost, and occasionally won. To those who had seen no advance until hundreds of their loved ones had "died in action" we must have sounded self-righteous, supercilious, and downright contemptuous.

One event stands out above all others in bringing us down to earth. We came to refer to it as our "Funding Fiasco." That was unfair, because this annual AIDS fund-raiser, organized by local businesses and supported by the public, showed the Philadelphia spirit at its best. We should have called it "our rite of passage." At the time it felt like a hazing. We hated living through it, but it forced MANNA "to grow up, get real, and show what our colors were like when we were up to our eyeballs in muck," as one sideline commentator said.

Once again we failed at something important before we learned how to succeed. Just like new lovers who dream of never falling out of love and parents who promise never to yell at the kids, we did what we vowed we never would: we engaged in an ugly, public, and counterproductive battle with a well-established AIDS organization, one we wished to have as a colleague. Failed vows are painful. It is hard to forgive an intimate who becomes the adversary, and it is even harder to forgive oneself for not avoiding the attendant recriminations. We had to do both, but the latter was the more difficult.

From the beginning, like all members of the AIDS community, MANNA was scrambling for resources. We felt compelled to create new funding streams and not attempt to siphon off any of the dollars other AIDS organizations relied upon. To us it made no sense to compete for resources. The overall funds available were insufficient, and every AIDS organization required more money than it had. Like all others we knew we had to conduct multiple fund-raisers each year, so we headed for new territory.

In 1990 an antique dealer came to MANNA with an idea for a fund-raiser to be called "Antiques for AIDS."[14] The proposal was that a group of antique dealers be asked to donate to MANNA 15 percent of the profits they received from everything they sold on the weekends in November. MANNA's contribution would be to organize this new affiliation of antique dealers, do the necessary advertising, and make sure as many people as possible made antique purchases from the participating stores during November weekends. If as many as twenty dealers could be recruited and the number of buyers increased by 20 percent, a conservative estimate of the money that could be raised was $20,000.

While this proposal had great appeal, it was going to be labor intensive, and we knew MANNA could not mount such an initiative during our first year. At the same time United AIDS Services (UAS), a well established organization in the city, had been contemplating making an overture to antique dealers themselves for a very different kind of fund-raiser. Over the previous months MANNA and UAS had been forging an alliance at the operational level and were in constant communication about many concerns. So MANNA met with UAS and decided to run "Antiques for AIDS" as a joint fund-raiser.

Since UAS already had in place major fund-raising capacities it was agreed that they take the lead role and that the proceeds be divided proportionally to the amount of work each organization did to raise the money. MANNA was to be the junior partner. For two years we worked well together. MANNA received 40 percent of the proceeds, a generous share considering what we contributed. In 1992 MANNA received $20,000 from Antiques for AIDS, nearly 5 percent of our income that year. The fund-raiser was a great success, and showed the promise of considerable growth.

This is our story of what happened to Antiques for AIDS and how our relationship with UAS exploded. I have been careful not to try to present the position of UAS because, apart from being unable to do it justice, I believe they alone should be author of their side of the story. My presentation here is simply MANNA's perspective on a very complex event, and I want to affirm that the experience of UAS in this conflict had an inherent validity, which we failed to grasp at the time. The purpose in this telling is to highlight what MANNA learned, not to throw dust in the eyes of people from another AIDS organization whose dedication, passion, and competence had been well proved long before MANNA's birth.

I am deeply grateful that the institutional wounds created by this falling-out did heal, that the leadership at both the board and executive director levels of both organizations became highly collaborative, that Antiques for AIDS continued to be a successful fund-raiser, and that many of our allies and adversaries who were hurt in the original fight became trusted and valued colleagues of both MANNA and UAS and distinguished themselves in AIDS leadership in many different organizations during the next several years.

So why tell this story at all? It was a profoundly shaping event in MANNA's evolution as an organization, and to omit it would be tantamount to whitewashing our history. It forced us to grow up. My recounting it here is designed merely to create a context for understanding the growth that came from what at the time was a devastating setback for MANNA.

By 1993 MANNA had built the capacity to organize events like Antiques for AIDS, and we decided to propose that we run years three and four of this fund-raiser and split the proceeds 50–50 with UAS. We wanted to be an equal partner. However, for reasons we initially did not understand, UAS seemed reluctant to meet and start the planning for that year. When we eventually got together, UAS opened with an announcement that they had taken out the copyright on "Antiques for AIDS" exclusively in their own name, that they wanted to expand the size of this fund-raiser considerably, and that the proportional amount MANNA was to receive was to be reduced.

Our immediate response was outrage! We did not think UAS had any right to claim exclusive ownership of "Antiques for AIDS." We felt betrayed and angry. We tried to communicate our distress, but the representatives of UAS we were meeting with did not seem to understand. UAS seemed surprised by our reactions but were firm. They said, "We have legal ownership of this fund-raiser so we can do what we like. We'd like MANNA still to be involved but on our terms. Please let us know as soon as possible if you are with us because we must get on with planning for the 1993 event."

Many AIDS organizations, struggling to survive in a severely underresourced world, behave like corporations jockeying for competitive advantage and battling for market share. Many thought UAS was just doing what was necessary and were telling us to "learn the ropes, to get our feet wet and our hands dirtied." We understood this. Our question was, "Is this the path for us?"

In the wake of this meeting, we considered several options. One was to fight UAS in court. Our legal counsel suggested MANNA would probably win, but this seemed pointless. Although the loss of this revenue was going to hurt, being in a protracted fight over something like this had no payoff. It would distract us from our primary mission, and since both organizations were serving the same people it did not matter if UAS or MANNA got the dollars; they were all being directed toward the same individuals. We felt we should keep our fighting spirits for the real battles: AIDS was a killer.

In my view, this was a war not worth having. However, some of our supporters argued that by having a good fight with UAS and demonstrating we could hold our own in a tough battle, they'd see MANNA as a worthy partner and be convinced we were willing to be part of the bigger cause.

The MANNA board ultimately decided to let go of the

Antiques for AIDS fund-raiser and to focus our collaboration with UAS on our mutual services. The question was how to do this without acrimony and without losing our shirt. It was not going to be easy. There were people in the HIV community who were angry with UAS and argued that it was MANNA's moral duty to take them on. Images of David and Goliath were all around us.

The major controversy was the administrative cost of this fund-raiser. In 1992, 30 percent of the total income from Antiques for AIDS went to administration. Many argued this was too high. This was one reason MANNA wanted to run this event for a while, to get this ratio down.

MANNA proposed that we gradually withdraw entirely from Antiques for AIDS over a three-year period. During that time we would contribute the same amount of labor as we had in the past, and in return we asked that MANNA's apportionment be maintained at the 1992 level (i.e., $20,000). However, we added two conditions: that administrative costs be lowered, and that the chairs of the two boards meet to sort out the relationship so the collaboration between the two agencies at the operational level not be hampered.

UAS, recognizing how upset we were, agreed to phase out our involvement. Thinking our main interest was money, they agreed to allocate MANNA $20,000 over each of the next three years, with one caveat: if administrative expenses were higher than expected or the total income did not grow as anticipated, the payout to MANNA's would be scaled back proportionately. They ignored the other concerns, which were the ones MANNA felt were the important ones.

As the weeks passed it was hard to bring this dispute to any amicable resolution. MANNA was perturbed that this struggle was becoming protracted. Unproductive emotions were creeping into all we did, sapping our energies. Recognizing that the conflict was beginning to undermine our work, the board decided to walk away from it entirely. We wrote UAS a simple letter saying that MANNA was withdrawing from Antiques for AIDS and would have no further involvement in it.

We felt great relief. The loss of the resources would hurt, but we thought this was the least damaging of the paths available.

But the fight would not go away. The fuse had been lit, and it was to explode whether we liked it or not. The next thing we knew the gay media was about to publish "that MANNA had elected to abandon Antiques for AIDS and had jilted UAS." The media called and read us what they planned to print unless we had a credible rebuttal. In essence it was that we had betrayed UAS and that MANNA was the villain in this debacle. Since the *Gay News* reached deep into the constituencies of all AIDS organizations, we were unwilling to remain silent. We told the media our side of the story, and suddenly our fight with UAS was in the public arena.

With this ugly exposé, the energy to fight seemed to dissipate. Several conversations were held between the leadership of the two organizations. We were both scrambling for damage control, and suddenly it was in both our interests to end the battle. My view was that if we did not stop fighting, the media would eat both UAS and MANNA alive.

We shied away from further joint fund-raising with UAS, but we did manage to work well with each other at the operational level. For quite a while, however, this fight left us overly cautious about partnerships with other agencies. This could have been a disaster had we remained stuck in this position. For MANNA to succeed it had to rely on its interactions with many other organizations and could not be isolationist or insular. The question was what type of partnering would best serve our mission.

We eventually came to feel okay about this fight. Other AIDS organizations recognized MANNA was coming of age. No longer was MANNA seen as trying to remain pristine. Getting into this political mess, which we had desperately wanted to avoid, taught us how to keep out of such situations in the future. Antiques for AIDS grew increasingly successful and raised many dollars for AIDS work in Philadelphia. And our donors showed us they were becoming more invested in MANNA by helping us make up the lost income.

The Birth of New Leadership

It was not long before the winds of change were upon us. First, one day, quite out of the blue, came a signal from the AIDS community that MANNA was being seen as a full and equal partner. A conflict among several other AIDS agencies had grown out of hand. MANNA's executive director was asked to act as a mediator. This request brought the clear message that MANNA was considered to have the strength and integrity to be respected by the warring parties. While we declined this request, it was an invitation to take up more of a leadership role in the AIDS world.

Second, in the summer of 1994 we were selecting an executive director to replace Gwendolyn, who had decided it was time to resign. David was the nominee of the selection committee and was voted by the board to fill the position. There was just one more step that had to be taken. David and I, as board chair, had yet to meet. The board instructed me to meet with him, decide if we could work effectively together, and if so, offer David the position in a way that ensured he accepted it.

I invited David to dinner with my family. My twin boys were six; my daughter was three: if he could survive a meal in my home, which was always a whirlwind, he could deal with MANNA's chaos. David passed that test fine. After retreating from the children we explored the issue upon which I thought my decision about David was going to swing. I told him what happened with Antiques for AIDS and followed it with a bold statement: "I want to keep MANNA away from the fights among AIDS organizations over resources." Without pausing to think, David, a decade and a half my junior, looked me right in the eye and said "Kenwyn, I totally disagree with you. MANNA must be at the table during these battles. If I become MANNA's executive director I'll be there every time. If we don't like how AIDS organizations relate to each other MANNA should get in there and work to find a better way."

Over the next hour he changed my mind, and before the evening was over I offered him the executive director position. I am very thankful that subsequent generations of leadership, at all levels of the organization, were able to guide MANNA into a full and collaborative relationship with the many Philadelphia AIDS organizations with whom we needed to interrelate. It would have been tragic for all concerned if MANNA had remained in a defensive and isolationist posture, for the reality is that in today's world virtually everything of value has to be done in interaction with others. I also admire the capacity of other AIDS organizations to accept that MANNA was able to learn from its mistakes while at the same time holding on to, and reinforcing, the values that made MANNA unique.

I smiled a couple of years later when David called from jail. "Kenwyn, I've just been arrested for protesting. As executive director of MANNA, I felt it was important to put us on the line. They will release me in a few hours, but MANNA is now on record that we will not stand for . . . ! Please handle the political fallout as you see fit."

I thought of our conversation when I offered him the job and the bumpy road MANNA took to become an authentic contributor in the cause of justice for those living with AIDS. For many of this generation, AIDS is what Vietnam was for mine. However, instead of an enemy far away in a place few could visit, it was in our own backyard, in a world most of us were unwilling to visit.

The Pain-Blame Cycle

Although the staff dismissals and Antiques for AIDS events were very different, contained within them was a common dynamic: one party was wounded by another, felt pain, and dealt with the hurt by looking for someone to blame. Having found a place to focus its blame, the offended party struck back, inflicting pain on the other and triggering a cycle with the capacity to repeat itself endlessly.

At a personal level I identify strongly with this tendency. Way back, perhaps in my childhood or possibly in genetic or social evolution, a knee-jerk response must have been coded into me: when in pain seek someone to blame, even before allowing all my own hurt to be fully felt. For most of my life it has been hard for me to see all the places this pain-blame trigger lurks within me, let alone find how to gain release from its imprisoning binds. Trying to break this nexus has been a big part of my inner agenda since entering adulthood. Of course, Buddhists teach that each of us causes our own pain, and that blaming another is a form of cursing the self. I find this to be a philosophically compelling idea, but when I think of actually putting it into practice I realize my heart still has much growing to do.

MANNA's internal and external battles forced us to recognize that we were not coping at all well with the pain that we absorbed from the AIDS community. The amount MANNA drank in every day was overwhelming. With each call requesting a meal, the first thing we were exposed to was the pain of the person asking for help, for each was desperate and hanging on to life by a shoestring. As we walked into each individual's habitat, we were blasted by the physical, emotional, and spiritual pain created by AIDS. Then, when one of our number died, we invariably sat with loved ones and shared in the shedding of tears for yet another snatched too soon from our midst. Whether we wanted this role or not, for MANNA to be MANNA, it had to be an importer of pain.

The issue was what were we going to do with all the pain we took in? Initially we did not recognize that we were in the "pain importation" business, and before even seeing this we were doing our share of spreading blame. We looked for those we could spray our unwanted emotions upon. We invented some repositories for these emotions ourselves and also borrowed from the list established by the HIV/AIDS community as a whole: blame government for all it hasn't done to stop AIDS; blame yourself; blame those who are spreading the virus; blame those who block free needles or free condom programs, etc.

Early on we were able to see in the behavior of others how counterproductive this pain-blame dynamic was, and we wanted to avoid doing the same thing ourselves. That's why we had resolved to keep out of AIDS politics. We appreciated that the in-fighting of AIDS organizations was just a way to block the tears, which people feared might otherwise never stop flowing because the pain of HIV is impossible to bear. And we didn't want to be part of this.

So what did MANNA do with the pain that came through its doors? We instinctively fought against being swallowed up by the angst of the AIDS epidemic because we were afraid we would become paralyzed, and paralysis would defeat our purpose. Determined not to let that happen, we did what every normal person tries to do, we emotionally distanced ourselves from the pain, both other's pain and our own. But, that didn't work. It just pushed the pain underground. Then it erupted, with volcanic force, through organizational fault lines we did not realize existed. And when it emerged, it was packaged in the same pain-blame conundrum we had wanted to avoid.

For MANNA to be MANNA it had to be an importer of pain, and we had to develop the capacity to own and deal with the pain inherent in the work we had taken on. But how were we going to become adequate containers of all the pain we imported? We had to keep ourselves connected to the pain without becoming anaesthetized to the anguish of those we served, to let the cursed side of life be in our face everyday, and to affirm the living contained within the dying. Until we could develop the ability to simultaneously grieve and work, without numbing ourselves to the pain, we ran the risk of seeking outlets for emotions we did not want to feel and becoming a contributor to the very condition we hoped to alleviate. Learning how to do this was a quite a challenge.

The Pain of the Desert

MANNA was caught in a dynamic similar to that of the Israelites in the desert. They had pleaded to be set free, but soon after their liberation all euphoria had vanished. The pain they wanted to leave behind had been so internalized it traveled with them and become more acute in the desert. When they were starving, the cry, "My God, my God, why hast thou forsaken us!" could not have been far from their lips. Apart from the pressing need for food, how would they cope with no enemy to blame? So they were soon to become their own enemy. They had already concluded that remaining in captivity would have been better than languishing on their own with no one to hold accountable for their plight. No longer able to condemn Egypt, they imploded, turning their anger on themselves. They started with Moses, berating their hero for even orchestrating their escape. "At least in Egypt we had food to eat," they moaned.

The biblical account gives no details of the acrimony they must have felt or the destructive things they said and did to each other as food was rationed and they fought over who was to be fed. Having seen this often in recent history, we can picture the scene. It was probably much like the Balkans in the 1990s, or the American Civil War, or the "killing fields" of Cambodia, or the once colonized African states ravaged by famine and battered by out-of-control warlords, or China during the so-called cultural revolution.

These wilderness people were in pain, real pain, which they could not tolerate and so moved into the pain-blame cycle. But their very future depended on getting beyond this. Imagine if the brewing revolt had led to Moses being killed off. Whom would they have turned to? Who would have stepped forward to lead them? Would it have become a process of endless scapegoating? Would they have fallen into a period of internal warfare? If we examine history, we see that one lesson humanity has yet to learn is how to avoid the civil war that occurs a few decades after a successful struggle for liberation. Was this to be the Israelites fate? How was this avoided?

The first answer is that, with Moses' help, they directed their blame at God, who held it and kept it contained. By so doing God interrupted, for a while, the ongoing pain-blame cycle. God's position was this: "If you have to export your pain, dump it in My lap. If you need to curse someone, curse Me. For if you keep placing more and more of your desert life under the curse, the future will indeed be bleak. Give me your curses, your blame, your pain," said God. "I will hold them and place them under the blessing. I will send you manna."

However, that was not the end of the story. The Israelites were instructed to grow up. They were not entitled to remain in this dependency state forever. Manna rained for forty years, but this gift came with the imperative that they become co-creators of the future. The starting point was that they had to develop spiritual muscles. That demanded a kind of exercise program for the heart, based on discipline and obedience to principles of a higher order than mere day-to-day survival. They were asked to live according to the Ten Commandments, the post-enslavement rules of civility given on Mount Sinai.

This proved to be a very bumpy road for these former slaves. Over the decades these lost souls designated to become the Almighty's chosen ones got into every conceivable mess. Moses often got fed up with them. Even God, it seems, felt they needed a long period of preparation, so long, in fact, that the original generation of liberated slaves had died off before the Israelites, God's people, were in a fit condition to enter the promised land.

Like the Israelites of old, MANNA had to accept that our long stay in the wilderness of AIDS was, in part, a period of preparation. And like them we never knew exactly what it was we were being prepared for.

Seven

DOUBTING OUR DOUBTS

Lesson 7:
MANNA changed how we looked at the world.

I LIKE TO BELIEVE that if I saw a truly great leader I would be among the first to follow. I doubt if I'd have followed Moses though. At least not initially. It's hard for me to accept things that stretch my credulity. Had I been tracking Moses from the beginning, I'd have started doubting his sanity the day he began talking about a bush being on fire but not getting consumed. Sure, it was early in his developing relationship with God, but hearing that story, any modern-day psychiatrist with American Medical Association accreditation would be thinking schizophrenia or LSD. And what does it say about those who elect to follow the village lunatic?

I also know that my wish for freedom would have been so strong that I'd have grabbed any opportunity to get out of Egypt, even if it meant tagging onto Moses. By the time we got across the Red Sea I would have begun to ask if I had misjudged him. Maybe I'd have reconsidered the plagues that had led Pharaoh to let the Israelites go: water turned to blood, frogs, gnats, flies, dead livestock, locusts, perpetual darkness, the death of all firstborns. These were surely dramatic displays of power. I'd have begun to wonder if there was more to Moses than first met the eye.

I do know that after I'd gathered manna for a while I'd have begun to doubt my doubts. At some point I'd have wondered what really happened with that burning bush at Horeb. And

I would have noticed that from then on Moses saw the world differently, that his eyes had become calibrated to see things the rest of us miss and that he saw every step he took to be upon hallowed ground.

The poet Elizabeth Barrett Browning captures perfectly the image of God being present in all of nature. In her epic poem "Aurora Leigh" she reminds us that every person sitting before a blackberry bush can see it as aflame with God. But most of us miss this reality. Only those with eyes calibrated to see this eternal truth take off their shoes. The rest of us just sit around and pick the berries off the bushes.[15]

My daily gathering of manna would have eventually altered my way of seeing the world too. I know this now because it happened before my very eyes. In Philadelphia in the 1990s hoards of people from all walks of life had their view of the world and their place in it radically altered by what happened at MANNA. Together we made several critical discoveries. They became our burning bush.

Finding the Blessing

Discovery 1: Feeling loved in one area of life infected all other parts. Even in the midst of extreme hardships it was possible to feel blessed.

One discovery MANNA made almost daily was that many of those we served, whose lives had been ravaged by disease, discrimination, economic hardships, and social injustice, actually felt blessed. This startled us. Most of us cooking and delivering the meals were still struggling for a sense of shalom ourselves. We were searching for a place where we belonged, where we felt valued, where we knew that what we did mattered, where we could feel heart connected to mind connected to spirit, where we knew the "peace which passes all understanding." We too yearned to feel blessed. Imagine how astonished we were to discover that we, who felt deep alienation in some important places within, were experienced by those living with HIV/AIDS as the carrier of the blessing.

This was how Linda expressed this idea. Those who delivered MANNA meals heard a similar story many times.

"Before I got sick I was a drug abuser," said Linda. "I didn't take care of myself. I do not know when I got the virus, probably '91. I got my diagnosis three years ago when I was forty. I was alone and bedridden. I was living in an abandoned building infested with drug activity. It was uninhabitable, and I was close to death. That's when I started getting MANNA meals. They've been coming ever since.

"My first experience with MANNA had a big impact on me. I remember the volunteer. Her name was Claudia. She came to my house in the evening. MANNA had called Claudia in the afternoon. They asked her to bring me a meal. It was too late to get a MANNA meal. So she bought me some Kentucky Fried Chicken.

"She came to my door. I told her to leave it in the hallway. She refused. She knew I was bedridden. She said she wanted to give me the food herself. I couldn't let her in. I felt too humiliated. I didn't want anyone see the squalor where I lived! I waited for her to go, but she wouldn't leave without seeing me. Finally I let her in. She walked into my room. She set up the meal and brought it to my bed.

"She saw that there was no food anywhere in my place. Without saying a word, she began making a list of the things I needed. When she was done Claudia told me she was going to the store to bring me some milk, bread, cereal, and other staples. Claudia stayed with me while I ate. She would not go until she was sure I was okay. After she left I began sobbing. I hadn't eaten in days. Claudia saved me from starvation. I was ready to die before she walked into my life. The next day she brought me three bags of groceries along with my MANNA meal. Claudia restored my faith in people and in life.

"MANNA's food is wonderful, but each day I look forward most to the volunteers visiting. They all sit with me for ten or fifteen minutes unless they are in a terrible hurry. Everyone asks how I am doing. They are all generous with their time and their words. I feel blessed to have such wonderful people looking after me.

"If MANNA had not been around I would be dead by now. I have no doubt about that. A lot of my increased strength is because of these meals. It is amazing. After I eat the food I feel much better. MANNA also has a nutritionist. I talk to her a lot. She helps me eat the right things not only because of the HIV but to control my diabetes and my weight. These meals not only saved my life. They have improved my health. I hope someday to repay MANNA for everything it has done for me.

"When I was first diagnosed I did not tell anyone about my disease. I was too ashamed. I wanted to die. I finally got my life together and stopped taking drugs. The first people I told were my children. I was afraid that they would hate me for having AIDS. They knew about my drug problem and were not surprised. They have stood by me and taken care of me. They live with me now. Once I got off drugs and got a little better it was okay for them to live here. I love those children. It is because of them my heart did not turn cold. They are everything to me.

"I told my mother about my AIDS just before she died. We had a difficult relationship. I am glad I was honest with her at the end. It brought us a bit closer. Other than my doctors and nurses, my god-daughter's mother is the only person that knows. My father and I have always been estranged. My parents separated before I was born. I only met my father after I was an adult. I told him I abused drugs. He said he was disgusted with me and wanted nothing to do with me. I never told him I was HIV positive. Black men don't want to know about AIDS. I have four older brothers and sisters. We never got along. I have a family that wants nothing to do with me. I often cry about it. They think I'm a dirty person because I used drugs.

"MANNA has become my family. Not only does MANNA bring me meals, they feed my children too. That makes me so happy. I cannot stand up long enough to cook a meal. I don't have that much strength. MANNA provides me with more than meals, though. One year they sent my kids and me to the play *Cats*. I remember my birthday the first year. The volunteer put my meal in the kitchen. Then she came out with a birthday cake and candles singing 'Happy Birthday.' I was so surprised and was touched that they remembered. At Christmas they brought a whole turkey with all the trimmings and dessert. My favorite thing though was last Christmas. They gave me the most beautiful picture, drawn by a child. It was the best gift I could have received. I still have it on my bedside table. That kindness I will never, never forget.

"I don't make my condition public. I feel uncomfortable having people know. People are very judgmental. I know more is understood about AIDS now, but people are still afraid of us. It makes me sad. We have so much to share. We have good in us that other people never see. I hope that changes. Not everything is bad for me, though. I have good days. Sometimes I have no pain. Then I can spend a little time outside in the fresh air. It's good to remember what life can be like. I thank God for every day I have on this earth to spend with my children.

"What MANNA does is God's work. When I get better, I want to work with them. I feel bad that I still need these meals. I've been improving, and I know there are others who are sicker than me. I pray for the people at MANNA every day. It doesn't matter if you are rich or poor; they will help you if you are in need. I am poor but I'd give them everything. It is the least I could do. MANNA saved my life and helped me believe again in people's goodness. MANNA gave me back my life and my faith. That makes me real happy. I still have many hardships, but I am more blessed than most."

When people like Linda told us their stories, we felt sustained. Yet we were also surprised. After all, MANNA's work was rather mundane. We went to the store and bought food. We took it to a central kitchen. We peeled and chopped hundreds of onions and carrots and potatoes. We baked cookies and brownies. We put gas in our cars. We drove freshly prepared meals to different crevices of the city. We knocked on people's doors. We dropped off the food. We sat and chatted for a few minutes. We asked simple questions like, "How are you doing today?" with no therapeutic or theological intent. And we were experienced as the carriers of the blessing!

Some who look at a blackberry bush see branches and leaves and tiny berries. Those infected by the way Moses saw the world take off their shoes and kiss the ground, for in front of them is a bush aflame with God.

Just as with the ancients in the desert, MANNA taught us that we do not have to go to the mountaintop or some holy place to be in the presence of God. Nor do we have to be a monk or a rabbi or a priest to extend the blessing. The most menial of tasks, done with love, are God's blessing.

Delighting in a Blizzard

Discovery 2: While we all hoped to avoid a life filled with crises, many critical lessons were learned in times of turmoil and uncertainty.

Since the day MANNA opened there was never any ambiguity about why we existed or what we were doing. Morning, noon, and night our energies were focused first and foremost on getting meals to those in need. No one ever questioned whether this would happen. It was taken for granted. If there were not enough volunteers to cook, the staff would drop everything and head for the kitchen. If a deliverer's car broke down, someone would jump into the van, pick up the meal from the stranded driver, take it to its destination, and circle back to help deal with the disabled car. MANNA's mission was simple and single-faceted.

However, the unequivocal nature of our mission, together with the variability in the day-by-day health of our clients, meant that MANNA was always operating with a crisis mentality. The number of meals required each noon could fluctuate dramatically depending on how many people had been hospitalized overnight, who was at an emergency medical appointment that morning, and who had a change in dietary needs due to the sudden onset of whatever. Moreover, any driver's schedule could be considerably thrown off depending on which Philadelphia streets were being dug up that day for emergency road repairs. While these fluctuations could be extreme, their unpredictability was normal. Even after five years, MANNA still looked like an organization trying to get its act together.

Those of us who were managers and executives in our other lives regularly scratched MANNA's collective head and made comments like, "This is no way to run an organization. We have to streamline our processes." We did our best, drawing upon state-of-the-art managerial and organizational thinking, and the staff put in place some innovative and enterprising systems for doing work. However, we never seemed able to move beyond a crisis mentality.

I'm not sure when it happened or exactly how, but there came a time when we stopped shying away from our crises. We did not look for them, but once we were in the midst of one we just dealt with it and let the important lessons contained within it come into our awareness in their own way and time. For MANNA a crisis became like a good muscle-building regimen for an athlete.

One of the most challenging and exciting times at MANNA

was a torturous week in January of 1996. One day a blizzard struck, and within twenty-four hours the city was blanketed by thirty-three inches of fresh snow. Cars were completely buried, and for a week all of Philadelphia was paralyzed. Roads were impassable, especially the side streets in poor neighborhoods that never saw a snowplow. That's where most of our clients lived. How were we going to deliver our meals? There was no question MANNA would be operating; the only issue was how.

It was wonderful to experience the elevated energy produced by the blizzard, along with the heightened creativity of the staff and volunteers who did what was necessary for the manna to reach all in need. That was God's commitment to those wandering in the desert: manna, their reminder that God was always with them, would be there every day, irrespective of the weather. We knew the sacredness of the original manna promise and believed we could do no less.

Although this was the hardest situation we ever faced, this blizzard was remembered as "the worst of times and the best of times." This is what MANNA did. Knowing a huge snowstorm was about to strike, the day before the storm we sent to all clients enough food to last two days. The day after the thirty-three–inch snow we reopened the kitchen and continued as normal. From the area hospitals emergency calls went out to anyone with a four-wheel-drive vehicle. The response was wonderful. Scores of people with vehicles that could traverse the roughest terrain on the moon voluntarily called MANNA to ask how they could help. The staff divided the city in half. On the first day double meals were sent to one section of the city and the next day to the second half. This way most people were covered.

That left just a few who could not be reached from our central location. Volunteers called all the clients to enquire how they were making out. When they learned that some, not scheduled to receive MANNA meals until the following day, needed food right away, they did what most people could never do. They picked up the phone and made calls to complete strangers living in the vicinity of the MANNA client. They boldly asked a simple question: "Do you have any extra food in your pantry or refrigerator that could be shared with a person living down the street who is too ill to get what they need for themselves." The response to these calls was extraordinary. Most were delighted they had been asked to help.

One MANNA client did go without food during the blizzard. An elderly woman, when asked if she needed food, said that for her food did not matter. She preferred that no one from MANNA risk life or limb for her. It was a greater comfort for her to know that the whole MANNA family was safe than it was to have a fresh meal. When asked in love, "Do you need a meal?" she answered in love, "I want to be sure everyone remains safe."

Despite this client's exhortation to be cautious, people behaved in the most tenacious of ways. One of MANNA's regular volunteers, a woman with an old station wagon, which was impossible to handle in the snow, was out each day making her regular deliveries. She got herself snowbound in some of the worst sections of the city. That did not stop her. She just asked whoever was on the street to push her car and get her on her way again. She managed to deliver all her meals and to get home successfully each day.

To an outsider, it seemed extraordinary how MANNA coped during this time. However, Steve, our volunteer coordinator, when asked what we did during the blizzard, replied with a perplexed tone, "What do you mean, what did we do? We delivered the meals! It wasn't easy. We had to figure out some things we'd never thought of before, but there was no question we would do it. That wasn't even an issue. Our job is crisis management," he explained, "and because at MANNA everything is a crisis, nothing really is. We are blessed and cursed by this twin reality."

From Grief to Service

Discovery 3: While it was not possible to repair what had been shattered, sharing our brokenness with others did provide a healing balm.

As a community we saw many loved ones die. AIDS has been a devastating killer. A question we have asked over and over again is "How do you recover from so much loss?" The answer is, "You don't!" The broken heart never gets to feel unbroken. The inner ache never disappears. The empty days and nights do not get filled again with joys long lost. There is no miracle cure. But, there is the possibility of a different kind of healing. It does not take away the aching but it does seem to place our brokenness under a canopy of the blessing. This was how John said it; for many of the MANNA community, this was their story too:

"I have been part of MANNA for three years. As a gay man I had always known about MANNA but never paid it much attention. But when my partner, Pete, became ill I wanted to learn how to cook nutritious meals for him, so I started volunteering at MANNA. I hoped my new ways of cooking would help him get better, but they didn't. I gave up cooking for Pete, and he started getting MANNA meals. Eating healthy increased the quality of his life, but it did not cure him as I had hoped. For a while, I felt bitter toward MANNA for not knowing how to save or cure Pete.

"I found at MANNA something different from what I expected. I have always felt alienated from a society that shuns gays and lesbians, and when Pete became ill I began to feel even more isolated. MANNA gave me a place to share my struggles. I found many other people who understood what I was going through and accepted me for what I am. In addition I discovered many volunteers who were neither gay nor had people ill with AIDS in their lives. I was touched that these people were working for MANNA. This surprised me and convinced me that the society as a whole was not as uncaring as I thought. I had never volunteered for anything before and started doing so for selfish reasons. These people, however, had different motives. Given the negative media coverage of AIDS, their caring surprised me. They helped restore my faith in humanity and encouraged me to start looking at the world in a different way.

"Pete had been my partner for eighteen years. He died a year ago, at forty-two. During the last weeks of his life I too received MANNA meals. I no longer had time to cook for myself. Tending to Pete took all my time and energy. I had never thought I would be served MANNA meals. That was such a help. After Pete died, I considered leaving MANNA but realized I had found a community that felt special. In addition to receiving support, friendship, and love, I could also provide others with the same. It gave me a way to carry on, to pick up my life. There have been many times in the last year when I was able to offer advice and comfort to others because of what I had been through. Sharing my own experience with others has made me feel a part of things in a way I never had before.

"Still, MANNA has been and continues to be a very important part of my life. I have a Ph.D. in English and had been a university professor. I dropped everything to look after my dying lover and discovered that college teaching is not nearly as fulfilling as caring for people who are needy.

"If I ever leave Philadelphia, the first thing I will do is to look for another organization like this, one that makes food for people living with AIDS. Preparing food is so intimate. When we make food for someone, we put a part of ourselves into the food, which in turn those who receive it put into their body. When you think this way you realize that this kind of giving is very personal and intimate, and you want to be sure it is done with love. Working for MANNA is a strange process. In some ways it is selfless giving and selfish receiving. In other ways it is self-full giving and self-full receiving. Whatever! It works for me. It restores me and makes me feel fully alive."

I love John's image of "self-full giving" and "self-full receiving." All of us of MANNA started with the belief that we would engage in "selfless giving" and were shocked to discover that each day we had also been "selfish receivers." Ultimately the idea of selfless and selfish gave way to a much richer one: self-full giving and self-full receiving expresses the part of God in each of us.

In Australia there are often bush fires that are so devastating that the scorched vegetation is seemingly lost forever. But in the months following the fire's destruction, we find that the searing heat that obliterated so much also brought back to life vegetation that had been lost the last time a fire of this intensity came by. It may have been as many as a hundred years ago. And that which is lost today may just be going underground for a hundred years, until the next intense fire brings it back to life again. Nature operates on cycles we mere mortals can only glimpse. Likewise, at times when we humans are subjected to great intensity, life lying dormant in us is brought forth in all its fullness.

Pete's death of course changed John and altered how he thought about his world and what was important to him. It could have left him feeling bitter and devastated. It didn't. His involvement in serving others brought to life capacities dormant in him, awaiting the arrival of the right catalyst.

One Day at a Time

Discovery 4: When we were in need of something, giving away what was in short supply quickly replenished the storehouse.

Two problems plagued MANNA in the early days. One was that our central facility, first the church and then our row-

house restaurant, was always brimming with people. We had
to decentralize certain functions, but the question was which
ones and when. Then once decentralization had occurred we
had to devise new systems of coordination. The first thing
we decentralized was the distribution process. We created a
number of meal distribution centers in the various neighborhoods where we had a large concentration of clients. One was
a church, another a florist, and so forth. At noon we trans-
ported all the meals to be delivered in that neighborhood in
large, heat-retaining vats. Then volunteer drivers and walk-
ers came to that center and took the meals to the MANNA
clients living nearby. A local volunteer or a worker at the
distribution center served as overseer of this process.

For example, one distribution center was a homeless shelter for families. At one point the executive director of that
organization became a member of our board. When asked
how being a distribution center for MANNA affected her
agency, she replied, "Everyone is enthusiastic about helping.
While at this time none of our population, young African
American mothers with babies, has HIV, everyone knows
the horrors of this disease and sees this as a way to help.
Each day we store the tubs with the MANNA meals in the
kitchen until volunteers come to pick up the food and take
it to people who live nearby. One day the tub was only half
full and one of the staff came to see me with a very troubled expression. She was worried a meal recipient had died.
I explained that meals weren't delivered when the recipients
were in the hospital or at a doctor's appointment. Her concern, however, was an indication of how MANNA touches so
many people."

The second problem was the difficulty we had finding
volunteers who shared the demographic profile of people receiving MANNA meals. We knew that for clients to derive
maximum benefit from their relationships with their caregivers it was best that, at least occasionally, those delivering

their meals were part of their community, where there were bonds that flowed naturally from the similarities of language, culture, race, ethnic background, and socioeconomic circumstances. For example, when Latino volunteers delivered to Latino clients, the link between MANNA and those we served grew stronger, and the relationships were easier to manage. Within a couple of years 80 percent of MANNA's clients were people of color and extremely poor, yet at the beginning most of our volunteers were white. We made some progress recruiting a more diverse volunteer pool, but this was difficult.

Ted, our vivacious and enterprising first distribution coordinator, organized one of the most exciting programs MANNA ever carried out. He established a relationship with "One Day at a Time," a recovery house for those with severe drug dependencies. Part of its program of recovery was community service. Ted persuaded One Day at a Time to allow the delivering of MANNA meals as an option for its community service requirement. From then on, MANNA's problem of getting volunteers in this region ended. The people in the drug rehab program loved doing MANNA work. Every day there were more than enough men and women willing to volunteer when the van pulled up at noontime. Tough-looking guys would even push and shove to get a place in line for the mere privilege of delivering a MANNA meal!

What was so special about this was the high level of identification these caregivers had for meal recipients. It drew these two groups of people who were needy in different and similar ways into a bond that enabled each to be helped by the other. Those whose hearts desperately needed to be healed became the source of help for others. And therein lay the redemptive cycle at the core of the MANNA story. We do not have to have our lives together to be able to make a significant contribution to others. In fact, those open to their own vulnerability, whose heart sat on some precarious edge, found it easy to embody and carry the MANNA spirit. The men and women at One Day at a Time drove this realization home to us all.

The fierce commitment and raw intelligence of staff like Ted, Steve, and Patrick led to many discoveries. Of course, from their perspective they were just looking for people who could help. But they found that the resources available to do the MANNA work were huge, once they learned how to tap the capacities of people normally shunned by society.

The Sacred in the Ordinary

Discovery 5: When unable to change what the world looked like, we were saved by altering our way of looking.

One day an artist and MANNA volunteer sent us a note that summarized how her way of looking had been altered by MANNA. When she and her husband decided to move to California, we published it in our quarterly newsletter.[16]

"Every day I think about MANNA. Why? Because chopping vegetables and washing enormous, almost-impossible-to-fit-in-any-sink pots have taken on a new meaning, a richer dimension.

"Before I started volunteering at MANNA one and a half years ago, I would chop vegetables for a specific recipe, the task at hand — dinner for six, lunch for three. Now when I chop veggies at home my mind floats to MANNA. Like Pavlov's dogs, I have been trained to respond to the experience. Washing pots isn't a chore anymore, a drudgery to avoid. The act of washing pots causes wonderful images and memories that well up in my conscious mind, recollections of Fridays and the MANNA kitchen crew — all of our jokes and conversation, concerns and problem-solving for each others' lives. I'm always reminded of the pathos of it all, the fact that we are doing these labors of love for people who are in great states of suffering and dying, people we don't even know, yet to whom we are fiercely devoted.

"It is this connectedness, this pulse of humanness that I eagerly look forward to every Friday. It comes in a strange way, through chopping and washing, ordinary activities that have become surrounded with deep emotions."

The question for all of us is this: Will we take off our shoes, or will we be among the number sitting around the bush, plucking blackberries?

Seeing in the Desert

Had I been one of the starving in the original wilderness I'm sure my vision would have been limited. As I complained to Moses I could have never dreamed of the response the Almighty came up with. When I heard the plan, sweet bread delivered each day with the morning dew, I would have suspected that God had lost His mind. Even if I trusted that the Lord was still functioning fine, I'd have argued that Moses had failed to read a critical section of the instruction manual.

The biblical account leaves no ambiguity that the people were being put to the test. They were asked to follow God's bizarre instructions delivered via Moses. I'd have failed that test. Given how many of my todays are spent concerned with things that won't occur until a distant tomorrow, I am sure I'd have been one of those who tried to stash some extra manna in my icebox. Then, the next day when I discovered the maggots, I'd have been writing to the CEO of the food company challenging Him on His failure to use adequate preservatives. What kind of a production system lets the food last only one day? Such contempt for standards!

I am equally confident that the weakest among us would be the first to say, "Just go with the program! If the prescription says only take enough for today, that's the wisest thing to do! The Good Doctor knows more about these things than you do." My point of surrender has always been one step shy of exhaustion. Those able to depend upon the Almighty before their inner reserves are spent get the spiritual nourishment long before the likes of me even realize our need for inner food. No wonder the One who Isaiah said would deliver us raised the issue of the last being the first and the weak being the strong.

The original manna story seemed so miraculous to the people at the time. But there is a sense in which it was quite ordinary. Imagine if the children of Israel had never seen a fruit tree, and instead of God sending the manna they had been told, "Find a tree, rest your weary bones, sit under its shade for a while, and one day you'll find ripe, juicy peaches, or long bananas, or milky coconuts to sustain you." If I were there listening to this, my primitive reaction would have been, "The gods must be crazy!"

Yet the reality is that every day for thousands of years we have all been fed by the fruits of nature. Before agriculture was developed our hunter-gatherer ancestors had discovered that God provided whatever they needed.

From my homeland comes a beautiful example of how the people learned to trust that the Great Spirit would provide. For fifty thousand years the nomadic Aborigines wandered in the Australian wilderness, what we call the "bush" or the "outback." They never carted water or food, for they trusted that Oneness, the Unifying Force of the Universe, would provide. When a kangaroo appeared on the horizon, the Aboriginal response was that the spirit world had informed this animal about some humans needing to be fed and it had volunteered to give up its life so others could survive. Hence, as it moved in the direction of the boomerang the kangaroo celebrated the lives that would be sustained as a result of its sacrifice.

This sacred image was part of every meal consumed by the ancient Aboriginal culture. The Aborigines, appreciative of the sacrificed flesh, first gave thanks to Oneness for providing the sustaining food and after the feast did not try to preserve any for the next day. Instead they made sure that a generous portion of the carcass remained so that other animals and birds could feast on it also. That way the whole of the natural order would be sustained. And if perchance no food showed up for a few days, they didn't worry but saw that as an invitation to fast for a while. Aborigines on walkabout ate only every few days. They knew that the body could go for a long time if they were patient and "waited on the Lord," as the Judeo-Christian tradition expressed it.

As a young man I had a powerful demonstration of this approach to food. I was working at a school in an Aboriginal village near the ocean. The first weekend I was there, the principal, who was leader of the local Boy Scout troop, invited me to join his dozen eight-to-twelve-year-old Aboriginal boys on a day trip to a local island. As we met early in the morning I was stunned to see that these barefoot lads had brought along no water and no food. As we climbed into the dingy taking us the five miles to a deserted island I asked the scout leader if I should get them some water. He knowingly smiled and said, "No, they'll be fine. Watch and see how the day unfolds."

Soon after we arrived at the island, one of the boys said he was thirsty. In a local dialect no white person had deciphered the twelve boys fell into an excited conversation. The next thing I saw was a boy shinnying twenty feet up a coconut tree. There were no branches to hang on to, and the trunk, a foot in diameter, was only five to ten degrees off vertical. Within a minute there were coconuts aplenty for everyone. A quick bang on a nearby rock punctured the hard skin, and they drank heartedly from nature's milk.

After a few hours of running around I thought for sure the boys must be hungry. I said nothing. Then suddenly all twelve of them took off in hot pursuit of a boar they saw lurking in the thickets. It took an hour for them to catch the wild pig, but they succeeded and quickly slaughtered it with a sharp rock they found in a cave. The boys dug a pit with their bare hands, filled it with twigs, started a fire by rubbing two sticks together, and three hours later were eating a feast of roast pork. They left half of the cooked pig lying on the ground and then sat at a distance and chuckled with delight as birds and animals emerged from the bushes to enjoy the manna that had been provided for them.

These Aboriginal boys knew the food for that day would be provided, so long as they were in the right spirit.

For forty years the Israelites were sustained by the manna, and by the time they reached the promised land reality looked different than it had as they were leaving enslavement.

MANNA also changed how we looked at the world, and after a few years I think we were collectively on the verge of realizing what Nelson Mandela worked out so powerfully during his twenty-seven years in prison, which he eloquently expressed during his inauguration as the first black president of South Africa in 1994.

"Our deepest fear is not that we are inadequate," said Mandela. "Our deepest fear is that we are powerful beyond measure. It is our light, not our darkness, that frightens us. We ask ourselves, who am I to be brilliant, gorgeous, talented, and fabulous? Actually, who are you not to be? You are a child of God. Your playing small doesn't serve the world. There's nothing enlightened about shrinking so that other people won't feel insecure around you. We were born to manifest the glory of God within us. It's not just in some of us: it's in everyone. And as we let our light shine, we unconsciously give other people permission to do the same. As we are liberated from our own fear, our presence automatically liberates others."

Eight

GROWTH AMID
TURBULENCE

Lesson 8:
To thrive in the midst of massive turbulence
required deep roots and radical shifts
carefully timed.

W HEN MANNA began we thought we would be in operation for only a short time. Surely science was on
the verge of some medical breakthrough, and HIV would soon
be cured. We did not think of our work as permanent. All we
would do was go out each day and gather some of the abundance existing in the larger society and deliver it to those in
need. We would be the manna gatherers.

That was not to be. Instead of being manna collectors and
distributors, we had to become the creators of an organization
with the capacity to function for a few interim years or maybe
for decades. This required the planting of deep roots and a
willingness to make radical shifts, delicately timed.

Growing Up

Initially there were so few of us at MANNA that everybody did everything. Roles were loosely defined, and staff
worked for low pay. After a couple of years we could see
that MANNA needed to do some institution building. The
growth in clients, volunteers, and staff was about to become

145

exponential. MANNA had to create job descriptions, develop personnel policies, establish salary structures, build a proper benefits package, and institute a performance appraisal system. Fortunately the early expansion of the board brought in new people with rich organizational talents. Many had years of high-level experience. At one point the board included three executive directors of major non-profit organizations, a vice-president for human resources of a large corporation, and a deputy commissioner of a major city government department. They helped MANNA put together a good set of personnel and managerial procedures without much trouble.

By year three, MANNA had the essential ingredients for an effective organization, an engaging, doable, appealing, marketable idea, solid financial support, and a high level of volunteer commitment. The most difficult issue was keeping everything in balance in the midst of all the changes that were going on simultaneously. This was most visible in the work of the distribution coordinator.

The responsibilities of the operations manager had been split and two new roles were created. One was volunteer recruitment, training, and management, which Patrick managed wonderfully for many years. The other dealt with the whole intake process and meal distribution: communicating with clients, case managers, and doctors, informing the kitchen daily about the number and kinds of meals needed, establishing routes for the meal distributors, organizing food deliveries, arranging the packaging of the food, and ensuring all clients got their meals each day. This role was gigantic in scope and importance.

Yet Another Godsend

Our first distribution coordinator after the operations manager left was Ted. He had been a MANNA volunteer and knew a lot about the possibilities and limitations of MANNA when he joined the staff. Using the foundation already established, over the next three years Ted built most of MANNA's infrastructure. During his tenure the daily number of clients grew from 50 to 350, and only in his last year did he have an assistant, Steve, who seamlessly took over and expanded upon what Ted had built when it was his time to leave.

Ted's brain capacity defied comprehension. His memory and ability to retrieve details at a moment's notice was phenomenal. He could spit out where every client lived, the best way to get there, each person's present medical condition and food preferences. He knew every volunteer meal deliverer, the condition of each one's cars, when they were available, and how reliable they were.

His interactions with the clients were so filled with caring that many thought of him as a best friend, even though most had never seen him face to face. During his service to MANNA, a few hundred of these "friends" died, and, with an aching heart, Ted was the one to inform the relevant deliverers of the most recent deaths. It would have been easy to treat each death as another statistic, another person no more in need of a meal. But Ted never grew numb to the realities and somehow drew strength from his sadness. Each death seemed to increase his commitment and his ability to function.

We knew that someday Ted would burn out. We could not predict when — at three hundred clients, at five hundred, at a thousand? After five hundred deaths, a thousand deaths? No one could go forever at his pace. His contributions were so staggering and he carried so much of the daily operation on his shoulders, everyone was completely reliant on him. We marveled at him, begged him to slow down, thanked him for all he did, and pleaded with him to get his processing systems computerized. Ted agreed, but never found time to do it.

One special challenge Ted faced daily was ensuring that

the kitchen and distribution operations worked in harmony. Nothing about AIDS is predictable, however, and he was constantly bombarded by chaos. He had to improvise every few minutes, making it hard to coordinate with the kitchen, but Ted managed everything well. For a long time, no one, not even Ted, could say what he actually did that made things work effectively. Certainly much of what he knew and did was hard to capture in a computer. It took two years for several computer experts who volunteered their services to create a system to capture the information stored in and processed by Ted's mind.

Every organization needs a Ted for periods of rapid growth. He thrived on the extreme demands placed on him and was able to produce order out of chaos. However, that only encouraged more and more of the turbulence of the external world to cascade inside MANNA's permeable walls. Life would have been easier had we kept more of the chaos out, but the MANNA heart demanded it be let in.

MANNA's building was always overwhelmed by the mobs of people arriving at noon to pick up meals. Our solution had been to create meal distribution centers in different parts of the city, places where volunteers would come to pick up the meals they were to deliver. Our first operations manager had started this system, and Ted enlarged it considerably so that when he left MANNA had twelve outlets for our meals in different corners of the city. As more and more sites were opened the pressures shifted. There was less turbulence in MANNA's building, which made things easier for most, but it added several new layers of complexity to Ted's role; he had to create ways of getting large numbers of meals to many places in a timely manner and had to manage more and more volunteers who never had face-to-face contact with him. Each step Ted took to relieve the pressures on others built more burdens into his role. Few noticed this, however, because he dealt with it so well.

Ted also displayed a shameless ability to beg. He had the uncanny capacity to get volunteers to do one more route or give a couple of more hours in the kitchen. Few ever said no to him, and yet he would get their commitment to give more hours without feeling put upon. Ted attributed his success at soliciting help to the volunteers' kindness, to their flexibility, to their commitment, to their generosity. He never noticed how he pulled this side out of us all, just by his own character. Ted knew that no matter how tough the situation was, MANNA would respond. His willingness to go the many extra miles, when body and soul were spent, showed that we could all do likewise.

We all marveled at how he could fly through the building and have meaningful two-sentence exchanges with whomever he bumped into, encounters that contained both work and personal significance. At his farewell party numerous people indicated that they had never had such a rich friendship with someone with whom they exchanged only ten-second sound bites. In fact for most of these "friends" his goodbye was the fist time they saw the holism of Ted's perspective on MANNA, captured in his farewell comments:

"I love the close-knit, caring atmosphere among the staff, the team orientation, the autonomy each person has, and the willingness of all, regardless of job title or level, to do whatever is necessary.

"I appreciate MANNA's diversity (only 50 percent of our staff is gay, compared to 80 or 90 percent gay in most AIDS organizations), the range of the ethnic, professional, economic, and social status of the volunteers, and the lack of sexism, racism, and homophobia at MANNA.

"It's interesting how few people used the support groups we offered. I think this was because every moment of every day at MANNA was like being in a perpetual support group.

"I'm glad MANNA never took our volunteers for granted, that we had special events to recognize them. MANNA's newsletter helped enormously in maintaining our volunteer base and making this a cohesive place.

"I'm thankful no one ever got hurt, given the rough places we go. That's possible only because MANNA is highly regarded in the community. We have no problems with thieves, thugs, or drug dealers, because the locals appreciate what MANNA brings to their neighborhoods and pressure the informal networks to protect us.

"My only gripe is the issue of salary equity, along with how few chances there are for vacation days. But this is such a client-driven place and not a person is here for self-interest, so it is easy to be forgiving.

"Working at MANNA has been one of the greatest spiritual experiences of my life. I've seen many very ill clients get healthier as a result of good nutrition."

Functioning with Grace in the Midst of Massive Uncertainty

To cope with all the peripheral uncertainty MANNA had to be deeply anchored at the core. Our faith provided that mooring. However, someone had to function as the chain keeping the turbulence at the boundary connected to the center. Gwendolyn, one of the original founding group, became our first executive director and operated as that link for several years.

A few months before MANNA began I asked Gwendolyn if she would consider serving as MANNA's first executive director. I am not sure I had the right to do this because we had not yet incorporated and no one had been assigned roles although it turned out that I was to become the first chair of the board of directors.

Gwendolyn let loose with her characteristically contagious laugh, and then looked at me as if I was crazy. "And exactly how long can you guarantee me a salary?" she asked jokingly.

"If we take the $4,000 First Presbyterian will give us, and if there's no major crisis, probably two weeks," I replied.

"That's more than enough job security for me," she dead-panned. "I am sure my husband will support my throwing away our family health benefits for a job with so much promise!"

When we got to discuss the proposal seriously Gwendolyn was both stunned and intrigued by the idea, but she did not think she had the skills. We reviewed her experience together, searching for clues as to whether this was a right fit. Three things were clear: (1) we knew some of the skills this position would require, but many of the prerequisites were a mystery; (2) if Gwendolyn failed the cost to her would be huge; and (3) if she was successful, the day would come when the role she created would be bigger than her capacity to fill it and she would have to quit. It looked like a losing proposition.

"Gwendolyn, it will require a leap of faith. You must sort out if this is *the* leap of faith you are to take," I concluded.

The idea of quitting her stable job and taking this position began to grow on Gwendolyn, and she decided to do it.

This was a tough job for Gwendolyn, and some situations stretched her close to the breaking point. However, it was the quality of her heart that enabled her to be successful rather than the executive skills she possessed, considerable though these were. There are many things about Gwendolyn I admire but most of all that she always doubted whether she had the experience, the skills, and the sheer human energy needed for this job. It was that doubt that kept her living in the "leap of faith" modality. So often Gwendolyn had to take actions in the midst of great ambiguity, where there was no indication of what the right path might be. What would she use as her guide? At the critical points she turned to her inner rudder. It required courage to take many little actions in the midst of uncertainty each day and then have to wait weeks or months for a clue as to whether or not she had made the right move.

There was nothing simple about Gwendolyn's role. Whenever she added someone to the payroll, she never knew where we'd find the money to pay that person. It was no secret that MANNA was living a hand-to-mouth existence, although we did make payroll every single month during the first seven years without borrowing a cent. Gwendolyn understood the look on the faces of new employees when they grasped the absence of job security at MANNA, for she lived with the same reality.

It was hard for Gwendolyn to gauge the quality of the job she was doing. On the one hand MANNA was being formed, hundreds were being fed, and MANNA's ethos was energetic, participatory, and transforming. Yet no matter how much money was raised, there never seemed enough, staff were worked to the bone, and the demands grew so fast we were always playing catch-up. Gwendolyn was always anguished to see one after another after another of our beloved volunteers who had the virus become ill and move from the ranks of the servers to the served. Such shifts evoked deep emotion. Gwendolyn was always there to be the container and carrier of those emotions when others found them too hard to manage.

One task Gwendolyn had to carry out as agent of the founding group was to organize the transition out of the church, literally and figuratively. We were determined to be nonsectarian, ecumenical, and inclusive, for both theological and pragmatic reasons. Ultimately the length of her tenure at MANNA was shaped by the timing and the character of that move; and the quality of her legacy was judged by how she effected this delicate shift.

Within months of starting we knew MANNA would soon outgrow the capacity of the church. Right away some started clamoring for a move and saw our slowness to act as evidence of incompetence. But we thought prematurely severing ties with our ancestral home could make MANNA needlessly vulnerable: our roots had to be allowed to go deep enough

to survive a major transplanting. Then when we did relocate everyone was busy establishing new modes of operating
so we could deliver on the growth this new facility made
possible.

Week after week, month after month, Gwendolyn, along
with her very skilled, organized, and compassionate administrative assistant, Emma, rode out the daily turbulence. These
were not tensions anyone could tolerate forever, however.
Even her successor, David, blessed with the energies of youth
and inheriting an organization already established, found he
too could carry out this task for only a few years. Once all
the basics were in place Gwendolyn and I began discussing
when to hand over the reins to new leadership. We thought
it best to do this when MANNA was in decent shape so
a new director could grow into the role without having to
deal with major crises, not that we knew when these would
come or the shape they might take. Timing of decisions like
this was critical, and a good portion of Gwendolyn's and my
shared energies were devoted to addressing the delicacies of
timing.

A few months after MANNA successfully moved out of
the church Gwendolyn felt she had accomplished what she
could and asked the board to find her replacement. She was
sad to leave behind the large family she had helped create,
but she knew it was time to pass on the leadership responsibilities to someone new. The farewell citation publicly read to
the assembled crowd at MANNA's 1994 annual art auction
highlighted her nobility of spirit.

*Gwendolyn, as we bid you farewell from your role as exec-
utive director we thank you for your part in this magnificent
gift we have all been blessed with, the gift of MANNA.*

*While it has taken literally casts of hundreds to create and
bring this organization to the fullness of its present life*

You have been MANNA's midwife,
   Your gentle arms have cradled us through the long
      and weary hours of the night.
You have been MANNA's nurturer,
   In the early morn your quiet voice has been there
      to encourage us as we wake from our slumber.
You have been MANNA's clarion call,
   Your stirred passions have compelled us to go labor
      in the field.
You have been MANNA's comforter,
   Your calming spirit has greeted us when our day's
      work has been done.
You have been MANNA's shepherd,
   its green pastures,
      its still waters,
         its overflowing cup,
            its staff and its rod.

Through you, Gwendolyn, the Lord's goodness and mercy
has been with us all.

Gwendolyn, you will always be in our hearts and we will
always be in your debt for the grace-filled and inspiring way
in which you have given us the greatest of all gifts — the gift
of your self.

Cooking Is All about Getting the Balance Right

Before we had the basics in place we realized that the crisis mentality driving MANNA would make it hard to do things that were radically different from our bread-and-butter operation. We knew this could be a long-term threat to our ability to be responsive to the HIV needs of the community. MANNA could become a stable, solid, and valued institution doing well its primary task but never grow into an organism that matched the evolving shapes and contours of this virus and its impact on people. We saw and understood this dilemma and debated regularly how to deal with it. But taking actions in the light of this realization proved harder than we imagined. Some initiatives that we undertook to ensure that we did not remain bogged down in our start-up history worked well; others did not.

Among our successes was that MANNA became expert at HIV nutrition. All our chefs and sous-chefs (Lisa, Griffin, Carl, Jenny, Brian, and others) made major contributions, and we reached the state of the art when our first nutritionist, Judith, arrived in our midst.

To explain the nutritional needs of those with HIV would require a technical treatise that would be out of place in this book. Suffice it to say that the wasting syndrome was hard to combat once it had set in, that at certain stages high protein meals were needed, while at other times high caloric intake was important, that those with conditions like diabetes required carefully tailored diets, and that the onset of diarrhea, mouth ulcers, and other conditions affected what one could eat on any given day. For many it was hard to take in enough food to get the needed nourishment, so eating had to occur in little bits all day long. This was especially critical for those taking protease inhibitors, for such medication worked only in tandem with the food being digested.

Since malnutrition suppresses the human immune system, the maintenance of lean-body mass was critical. In fact the quality of the nourishment of those with AIDS was probably a better measure of morbidity and mortality than an individual's blood count.

Within a couple of years the MANNA kitchen expanded its operation greatly: each person could select from forty permutations of nine daily meal modifications, depending on presenting symptoms; the deliveries were increased from one to two meals a day; Saturday meal preparations and deliveries were commenced; and we expanded to three kitchen shifts a day, beginning at daybreak and ending when the work was finished in the evening. The earlier conflicts between the kitchen and the distribution process vanished. It was not that the tensions lessened. They actually escalated, in concert with the growth in numbers. But the expansion of the demands upon us changed the climate of MANNA, and we all started to bring out the best in each other. Just like with a good meal, the commitment and capacity of the staff to maintain a sense of balance contributed to MANNA's success.

Eat Well, Think Well, Feel Well

Another big leap for MANNA was to appoint a full-time nutritionist. Judith was a well-established professional when she joined the staff in 1994, and within a short time she was offering a host of gifts to the AIDS community through MANNA. She established and became our first director of Life Span (Support for People with AIDS through Nutrition), a program of nutrition counseling for people with AIDS, offered freely to those residing in Philadelphia and the nine surrounding counties.

Judith did the counseling via phone, in the MANNA offices, or in clients' homes. Traditionally nutritionists had not made home visits, but doing so proved very useful. It helped Judith to offer advice that fit the nutritional possibilities of each individual's habitat and provided a level of confidentiality essential for our clients. The counseling concerned how to maintain body weight, how to get the right mix of major vitamins, and how to ensure food safety, an essential for all with HIV. She also offered information about which food relieved various symptoms, the best exercises for those limited by the virus, herbal remedies, medical referrals, dental care to avoid infections, and the relevant psychosocial support.

One of her greatest contributions was the production and publication of a book called *Eat Well, Think Well, Feel Well,* a nutrition guide for persons living with HIV/AIDS and their caregivers. This publication filled a significant void in the accessible, relevant information on nutrition and HIV. Tens of thousands of copies, at extremely low cost and in many cases free, were distributed nationally the first year after its publication. Within months of its release, the National Institutes of Health selected it as the nation's standard for HIV nutrition education. Subsequently the book was issued in Spanish and was reedited for compatibility with the food preferences of specific ethnic groups.

Judith was also MANNA's nutritional outreach ambassador to the larger AIDS world. She could regularly be found at other AIDS organizations giving talks about nutrition, writing articles for their newsletters, and visiting any place willing to hear about the importance of nutrition for those with HIV/AIDS. While AIDS was her focus, Judith actually had a larger mission. She was eager to improve nutrition for all, and anyone who listened to her left thinking about their own food intake in new ways. Her work showed the world that MANNA was for all, and not just for the HIV/AIDS infected/affected.

The decision to institute Life Span represented a change, an extension of MANNA's mission. Moving from just providing hot meals to the homebound was something we had wanted to do from the outset. We always believed we had to assist those with HIV long before the onset of malnutrition. LifeSpan was MANNA's first successful foray into the prevention rather than the correction of nutritional deficits.

While Judith had her own specialized niche, she fully embraced the whole of MANNA's work. It was quite common to see her pouring punch for the children at the annual Kids Care reception, donning an apron as part of a kitchen crew, or making an emergency meal delivery, along with the other staff, when some urban crisis meant not enough volunteers were able to get to MANNA that day. She felt the MANNA she joined in 1994 to be the best place she ever worked, but in truth she was one of the people who had made it such a place. Judith both appreciated and contributed to its being an agency filled with intelligent, hard-working, caring, dedicated, humorous, vibrant human energy.

Not Doing as Much as Was Needed

MANNA seriously contemplated three other programs at different times, with the goal of preventing rather that reversing malnutrition. We implemented two but only one was successful. The one never set in motion remained but a dream.

First, the unsuccessful one. MANNA began offering cooking classes for people living with HIV and their caregivers. This was a fine idea, but we tried to implement it when the demand for meals was growing at a relentless pace. In the same period, we were also overwhelmed by two key events, moving from the church to our next home and then the chef's dismissal. MANNA's cooking classes fell by the wayside. Before we were able to consider restarting them, our former chef had established a new life and was successfully running cooking classes for this same group elsewhere in Philadelphia. Hence the need for MANNA to do it had faded.

The one project we never got off the ground was "MANNA TAKEOUT." The idea was that people with HIV who had enough energy to hold down a job but not sufficient to cook a nourishing meal at day's end would be able to call and order a special MANNA meal, just like they might for any other takeout food. We thought we could make available to them high quality MANNA meals, carefully prepared by loving hands, as an alternative to something quickly prepared by teens making $5 an hour at a local pizza joint.

The successful program was the introduction of meals for large groups of people. These took place in various settings and in collaboration with other Philadelphia AIDS organizations. Once established, each week hundreds of MANNA meals were consumed by HIV positive folk who were well enough to assemble in a church hall or any other suitable place. In 1996, 879 people received home meals while 1,891 ate at congregant meal locations. In 1997, the number of homebound recipients remained steady while the number of congregant meal recipients grew to 4,518.

A Crisis That Never Happened

In 1992 we asked ourselves how we would handle a worst-case scenario, like the number needing meals suddenly jumping by a factor of ten. With thirty thousand infected Philadelphians and an expected incubation period of ten years, unless there was a major medical breakthrough, three thousand could die each year. We guessed we might need to feed about 10 percent of these people during the last year of their lives, about three hundred. That proved to be a realistic assessment. But what if some strange set of socioeconomic forces or the arrival of some unexpected, unknown opportunistic illness meant we had to feed 50 percent? Could we respond?

We thought the need to build a large distribution system quickly could cripple us. In crises like famine and floods, the biggest problem is usually distribution. We were confident we could make the meals and believed the money needed for such an expansion would be forthcoming. However, getting a dramatically expanded distribution system in place quickly would be a problem. To quietly prepare for such an eventuality we started partnering, in other areas of MANNA's life, with organizations that had fleets of cars cruising the street all the time and for whom delivering a few MANNA meals while doing their other tasks would be no hardship. We targeted three organizations.

First, we formed an alliance with the visiting nurse associ-ation. The primary reason for this partnership was that these nurses were well positioned to assess the fluctuations in the

nutritional needs of our clients and to deliver advice on nutrition for those with HIV but not in daily need of MANNA
meals. This agency also had a large number of cars crisscross-
ing the city at any time, and we believed that, if needed, they
could easily drop off MANNA meals as they visited the homes
of those with AIDS.

Second, we vigorously sought funding from CoreStates
bank so that it would be constantly informed about MANNA.
The bank had scores of corporate cars parked in the base-
ments of several skyscrapers, most of which sat idle at
lunchtime. CoreStates had a strong community service focus,
was working to embrace the diversity of its workforce, and
was trying to combat racism, sexism, and heterosexism in
the bank. We believed that if a distribution crisis occurred,
CoreStates would let its employees use company cars to help
distribute MANNA meals.

The third organization with many vehicles was the Red
Cross. There were many reasons to ask the chief executive of
the Red Cross to join our board, which he did. This man had
vast knowledge about organizing emergency services, knew
everybody, and was in a position to open many doors for
MANNA. One that could be most helpful if our worst-case
scenario became reality was access to Red Cross vehicles
racing around the city dealing with human crises.

We also discussed many others who were continuously in
their vehicles, like undertakers, real estate agents, firefighters,
and UPS delivers.

Mercifully none of this ever became necessary, but we were
determined to be prepared to take fast action if our worst fears
were ever to be realized.

Growing Pains

There was nothing simple about MANNA's maturation process, given the level of uncertainty we faced. We made

mistakes and recovered, fell into organizational traps and then got out of them, took three steps forward and two backward. We were a lot like the Israelites in the desert.

When I was young I often wondered why the Israelites took so long to reach the promised land. Were they incompetent travelers? Was their leadership unable to mobilize them? Were they going round in circles? By midlife I came to see that they, like me, were works in progress, for whom the term "finished" would never apply and hence had no meaning in chronological time. If one moves to a cosmic version of time, the beginning is the end, an instant is infinity, the last second is the first. Then one gets caught in a logical tangle where the concept of time collapses and the only moment is the eternal now. In that frame, the validity of the old adage "the destination is the journey" is self-evident, and the promised land ceases to be a place to be reached and becomes a way of being that is open to being reached. Suddenly forty years, no matter how wearying it might have seemed, was rather short.

While their journey seemed to be taking them nowhere, the Israelites did receive the quintessential revelation for both human civility and divine connectedness, the Ten Commandments. But their moments of amazing revelation did not set them on a straight path. They got into all kinds of trouble and had to be dragged, kicking and screaming, into the rights and responsibilities of being the free.

One problem was that some of the commands they were to obey defied rationality. Consider the "no accumulation" rule[17] (stockpile manna and it will rot and breed maggots), a motif picked up by Jesus in his prayer, "give us *this* day, our daily bread" not "give us *today tomorrow's* bread." In short, this lesson was that the goodness of God can't be stored up. It must remain in constant circulation.

Then there was the instruction to gather a double portion on Friday so the sabbath could be a day of rest. Attempted accumulation fails, but one day in seven it works, but only for twenty-four hours, and only if you do it on the right day! I can identify with those who did not follow the manna rules. Not only would I have exclaimed loudly, "What is this?" (*mon hu* in Hebrew: "mon," or "manna," in English)[18] the first time I plucked the sweet bread off the dew-covered ground and gingerly tasted it. I'd have tried to hoard it and then yelled again "What is this?" when the rot set in. I'd have also skipped Friday's double pick-up and gone out on Saturday for my daily ration. Upon finding nothing I'd have let loose with a bitter and incredulous "What is this?" once more. Even then, I'd have tried a double dose on Monday intent on making Tuesday my day of worship rather than the sabbath as instructed, and found "What is this?" on my lips again as God failed to fit my image of what the Almighty should be like.

In concrete terms, manna was Israel's breakfast each morning for forty years. "Without variety," a restaurant critic might add. But manna was more than just the bread to be picked up each morning from the "Cosmic Bakery" or "Bagelnosh." It was the assurance that God had not deserted them. They had to feel abandoned, however, before they could know what it was like to feel not abandoned, one of the great mysteries of the spiritual world. How does one know that this invisible God is nearby, as close as the breath that fills the lung, unless we can also feel God's simultaneous far-away-ness. If God were visible to us all the time, we'd begin to think of the Almighty as one of us, as no longer God, and that just might lead one of us to erroneously think we were god!

As they picked up this strange substance, the Israelites exclaimed, "What is it?" It is only those who are confused about "what it is" who receive the manna. It is in the "I don't know" that one becomes open to the knowing which is based upon, but transcends, the not knowing. For the ancients, manna was the confusion and the clarity, the lostness and the foundness.

Did the wanderers in the desert ever figure out what manna was? Probably not. But when they ate it they were sustained, so why be paralyzed by the "what is it?" question any more? Quite a metaphor for the spiritual life. Certain things nourish the spirit, even though we don't know how or why. Those who recognize this come and eat.

Had I been a child of Israel I suspect it would have taken me years to get with the program. And I'd have uttered, "What is this?" so often, it would have become my refrain. Of course, I'd have also failed to notice that saying, "Manna, what is it?" "Manna, what is it?" "Manna, what is it? ..." again and again was actually becoming a litany of praise spawning my growth in deeper places and not just a lament revealing my surface resistance. Submission, easily offered, is shallow, but surrender in the exhaustion of rebellion comes from the Job-like depths. I think the manna story, along with the children of Israel's endless detours that lasted for forty years, tells us that God understood this well.

Nine

HEALING THE BREACH

Lesson 9:
MANNA both sharpened and healed
the tensions of race and social class.

During the first few years at MANNA we had to wrestle with a variety of social "isms." In some areas we did well. For example, social class did not appear to be raising its ugly head: MANNA served the wealthy and the poverty-stricken without charge and without attending to the recipient's social standing; rich and poor worked side by side in the kitchen, without anyone even noticing who belonged to which stratum of society. MANNA did well on the issue of age: we had high school students and the elderly appreciating and happily reinforcing each other's energies. For the most part, sexual orientation seemed inconsequential. That was special because when MANNA began the hostility toward gays and lesbians was still palpable in most settings. The religious right was strong, mainline denominations were debating what status to afford gays, lesbians, and bisexuals, and the U.S. military would not even permit public acknowledgement of one's homosexuality.

The ism that caught us most by surprise was racism, especially as we tried to diversify the board. This distressed us because we fell into a classic organizational pattern. We even noticed what we were doing but seemed unable to avoid it, much to our chagrin.

Diversifying the MANNA Board

MANNA had emerged from a predominantly white church, and the initial leadership of our young organization was all white. We were balanced in terms of gender, age, and sexual orientation, but we knew we had to become racially diversified. This proved to be a more difficult process than we imagined.

We discussed the importance of including African Americans and Latinos in our ranks even before we opened MANNA's doors. But there were many items on our top priority list, and we let our concern about our whiteness fade in importance, agreeing to address it as soon as MANNA started. Also, in the late 1980s, the majority of those who had publicly acknowledged having AIDS were gay white men, so we did not give race the attention it deserved. We did, however, have some very enlightening conversations with the black clergy, the core of the black leadership in Philadelphia, and felt well positioned to address this issue in 1990 or 1991.

In late 1990 we began recruiting new board members. We approached both Latinos and African Americans. It turned out that a large number of the people we were serving were poor and people of color, and we had to open ourselves quickly to many concerns whites don't usually consider. One Latino did agree to join us, but we were not successful in bringing any African Americans onto the board at that time. We went back to the black clergy and asked for help in finding leaders in the African American community to serve on our board. As a result, one black man joined us but he soon dropped out. We had hit a brick wall. MANNA was still a tiny organization with no visibility and the demands placed on the black leadership were so high that they had to be selective about where to place their energies.

We were disappointed. Frustrated by our failure to diversify our leadership ranks, I approached Pearl, an African American

woman who was a highly experienced organizational consul-
tant. She joined the board but found that what she had to
contribute to MANNA was undervalued. This was how she
expressed it.

"I was so impressed with MANNA to begin with. When I
ate a MANNA meal I thought the clients were sure to stay
strong if they ate this delicious and nutritious food each day.
I decided to come aboard. I eagerly embraced my role as a
newcomer, but it was hard to connect with all that was going
on. MANNA was still located at the church, and the other
board members knew each other well. They had strong bonds,
knew the culture of MANNA and the community they were a
part of creating, and were operating a fast-moving, extremely
chaotic organization. It was hard for me to find my place.

"As I looked at the board as a whole, I began questioning
why there were no other blacks and asked myself if I had been
recruited to serve as *the* black representative? This made me
feel very uncomfortable. I felt burdened by being the only
representative of my race on the board. Soon I was caught
up in that all-too-familiar minority dynamic. Everything I did
at MANNA was framed by this position I was occupying as a
representative of my race. For example, if I were running late
for a meeting, I'd wonder, 'If I'm late, will that reinforce the
stereotype that all black people are late?'

"I recognized that others on the board were not thinking
about this. The fact that it was not in their awareness but was
always in mine made me feel even more isolated. After a year
or two I still felt like an outsider. I wasn't making enough of
a contribution to justify occupying a seat on the board or to
spend my own time this way. I decided to resign. At a board
meeting I explained why I was leaving, that it was just too
tough being the only representative of my race on the board.

"After I described my experience one member said, 'I always
wondered what your purpose being here was, if you were *the*
black on the board.' That one comment validated my impres-

sions. The full range of what I might have brought was being stifled by my being the only person of my race in the group."

After Pearl resigned we asked her to lead us in a discussion of how best to diversify MANNA's leadership. By this time our sole Latino board member had also left, although ostensibly for different reasons. As board chair, I was eager to have this conversation and was also anxious. I knew how hard these conversations could be, especially if approached defensively. I wanted us to talk about race without falling into the pain-blame dynamic we spoke of earlier. I knew Pearl was not blaming us, but she was telling us about how painful it is to be black in a mostly white world and to have whites be seemingly oblivious to this reality. I hoped we would not try to avoid her pain by falling into our own, by becoming defensive, or by blaming blacks for not stepping forward to fill the leadership roles we wanted them to occupy.

The conversation was very constructive. Several board members expressed regret that MANNA had not been able to use her very considerable talents and thanked Pearl for the advice she was offering us. We focused on what it meant to have no representatives on the board who were African American, Latino, or Asian, since so many of those we served were people of color. We did not fall into the familiar cycle of pain-blame-pain. We recognized we weren't to blame for the racial hole we were in, but we had collective responsibility for getting out of it. The reality was we had failed to build a racially diverse leadership group, but acknowledging this without judgment or blame let us get on with the task before us. We resolved to accept Pearl's counsel, to bring several black members onto the board at the same time. We also agreed to address the lack of Latinos on the board but decided to take one step at a time. For the immediate future recruiting African Americans into the leadership of MANNA was our top priority.

As we searched for black board members we came across

many wonderful people. Some said no. Others said yes. In the next two waves of board recruits three out of five and four out of six new board members were African Americans. This proved to be a most successful way to approach the task of diversification. In 1995, six of the twenty-one board members were black and the range of skills and professions brought by these African Americans was quite varied. One was a lawyer, another had been a legislative aid to a politician before becoming a MANNA client, one was a physician, one was a retired medical school professor, one was a nurse working in a mental health center, and one was a housing specialist with the city. Two were women and four were men. In 1996, two of the five members of the board's executive committee were African Americans.

Ultimately diversifying the board in terms of race was not all that difficult to achieve. Once again, however, MANNA had failed before it succeeded. We had dealt with race tokenistically. What was so frustrating about this is that we had enough understanding to have known better, but we made this mistake anyway. Although this was painful for Pearl and for the board, which once again had been tripped up by our limitations, it worked out well.

The African Americans who came to MANNA made many great contributions. As they served they also brought the kind of energy that actively contributed to the lessening of the painful race relations in Philadelphia.

A Black Volunteer Speaks Out

One of our African American volunteers spoke eloquently and passionately about this issue. "I've been volunteering at MANNA for ten months. Over the previous seven years I'd volunteered as an 'ActionAIDS buddy' to three men living with AIDS.[19] They all got MANNA meals, and I was often there when the food arrived. We were polite, but I felt indifferent about the MANNA volunteers. However, when one of my buddies was in the hospital I had to call and tell them not to deliver food that day. The person at MANNA answering the phone told me to say hello to my buddy and to wish him well. That morning I personally felt MANNA's warmth and concern. Then a few weeks later when another buddy was having a birthday, MANNA sent a birthday cake with his meal. Little things like this say a lot about an organization. After my third buddy died I wanted a new role. I started working in the MANNA kitchen on Monday nights.

"I have learned so much from AIDS. But the biggest lesson for me, as a black man whose buddies were white, has been to see how this disease has brought people of different races together. On his deathbed one of my buddies said he never thought a black man would be reading him stories when he was dying. When his parents met me at the funeral, they were startled to realize it was a black man who had voluntarily given hours a day to help their son over his last few weeks. That's all part of it. At death's door we are all equal, we are all the same.

"My connection with AIDS started in college. As a freshman I was lost. I was scared and nervous and felt I didn't belong when I was befriended by Dr. Wellford, a young white assistant professor, who helped me through some tough times. He became my mentor at college. For several years we lost contact. Then one day he sent me a postcard. He was living in Washington, D.C. As a lawyer working for the Justice Department I was in D.C. regularly, so I met up with him again. That's when he told me he had AIDS. We talked at length about his illness, and before he died, Dr. Wellford urged me to work as a volunteer for organizations serving people with AIDS in Philadelphia. This conversation led me to start volunteering. It was my way of keeping my mentor alive within me.

"Most MANNA volunteers have a story to tell about someone they've lost. As we do our tasks we work out our grief and honor someone special in our lives, by giving to those going through a similar experience as our loved one. As we work side by side with each other we know intuitively that we are all working out our relationship to the disease. We've each been affected by it, even though we may choose to keep our specific stories private.

"MANNA feels safe because it gives me a chance to do something without being on the front line. It also gives me a way to be serious without feeling serious. Chopping vegetables and packing meals side by side with others is relaxing. We have fun together, and we enjoy ourselves. Yet it is critical that we do it right and efficiently. We must pack the correct food in the right containers. It's not like packing thirty lunches for kids going to the zoo. When I am working at MANNA I am very focused regardless of the stresses in my life at that moment.

"To begin with I had a difficult time breaking into the inner circle with my kitchen shift. Some of them had established strong bonds, so it wasn't easy, but slowly I became friendly with most. There are always little problems that we have to work out, but overall it's a caring place. MANNA's strength is its simplicity. We do one service and do it well. Everyone knows what has to be done, and we just do it. MANNA cannot make the disease go away, but it makes the lives of people much more manageable, day-to-day.

"Kitchen workers have no direct contact with the clients so none of us do it for the personal accolades. We're anonymous. The people receiving the food don't know we prepared it. For a variety of reasons most of us in the kitchen couldn't emotionally handle direct contact with the clients, but we help in an indirect way.

"I now see there is a strong spiritual component to what I'm doing. As I grow older, going to church is not a sufficient way to express love for God. Doing things for others is the true thanksgiving to God. Working at MANNA is my spirituality in action. I'm glad I can write a check and donate money to charities, but giving my time and my heart is more important for me."

In the desert manna was a healing force, a daily reminder that the abundance they had been given was sufficient for that day. It was the same at MANNA. In the 1990s the MANNA community included many races and creeds, yet all felt the same spirit. Over and over the pain created by our historical differences was gently soothed by whatever hand was being lovingly extended at that moment.

We loved to hear this, especially from our clients.

Jeb's Last Few Months

For many with AIDS, the last months were filled with set-backs. The quality of any day could be colored by the onset of blindness, dementia, continuous vomiting or other complications. When we talked with Jeb he was delightfully lucid, given that he had begun his descent. He jumped from idea to idea, but had a Forrest Gump–like coherence. He said that the spirit of the people around him had a major effect on his life, that he felt cared for by MANNA, and that he was enriched by having MANNA volunteers who were of different races and nationalities. He died a few months later.

"I live with my partner, Rod. We both have the virus. We get MANNA meals. The food helps him a lot. He has a part-time job. He's not real sick. I've been getting MANNA meals for two years. I am mostly homebound. I like it best when the volunteers visit. Some are black, Hispanic, white, and Greek. They are all good people.

"Today was my grandfather's funeral. I didn't go. My mother and everybody will be angry with me. I hate funerals.

"MANNA is great. Steve [the distribution coordinator] is real nice. He calls all the time. He checks up on me. This

Thanksgiving the meal was real good. At Christmas they sent a card made by a kid. It had a nice picture on it. The meals have improved a lot. I've always liked the dessert. Some of the meals were like eyeballs. The main part is good now though. They could use more seasoning in the food.

"MANNA volunteers greet us with a happy face. I like that. I can smile good too. They must like their work. One time the bell was ringing and ringing. I was nasty with the volunteer. He got nasty back. I felt bad. It wasn't his fault. The bell was stuck. I reported him to Steve. The next time he came he was real polite. He even called before. He wanted to check if the bell was working okay. That was real thoughtful.

"I don't walk anywhere now. Rod walks all over the place. He walks all the way across Philadelphia some days.

"MANNA people are real hospitable. They bring good spirit. If they get a cure for AIDS, MANNA shouldn't stop. I like it when the volunteers come. They are all good to me.

"My brother just died of AIDS. He got sicker quicker than me. My mother just got bypass surgery, on top of everything else. It took Rod a year to tell his mother he had AIDS. She still hasn't got used to it. My family has been okay. My older brother is retarded. He gets along pretty well. My younger brother didn't even make it to twenty-seven. I'm not ready to die. I make every doctor's appointment. I take all my pills.

"It's a sin to be gay. That's what my uncle says. He's a minister. I try not to be gay. I'm tired of dealing with it. I used to live at a place infested with AIDS. A friend had lost lots of weight. Rod went to help him. Found him dead. He had been dead for days. He smelled awful. It was terrible.

"Section 8 housing came through for me. Praise be to God. I was paying $124 a month. Now it's $40 a month. They cut off my cable TV. I couldn't pay the bill. They wouldn't give me more time. I only needed a week. My last landlord was real nasty. I had to pay security guards to protect me! I'm glad to be here.

"I'm worried about Rod. He won't go to the doctor. His blood count is down. My white cell count is down too. It's relationship stress. I must ask Rod to leave. He's crazy. It's killing me. I never forget my pills. I ask my doctor lots of questions. He says to always take my pills. Then I will last forever."

An Angel with Leg Braces

At the time of MANNA's dedicated effort to increase the racial diversity of our board we also intended to include some of our clients. Jefferson, an African American man in his forties, was one of the first people we approached. He accepted, and for many years served as an insightful and forceful member of our board. During that time he also worked as a MANNA volunteer, and when he was too ill to care for himself he received MANNA's meals. During his time on the board he ensured that we listened to the voices of those normally ignored.

Jefferson also taught us to respect all kinds of diversity, not only those born of race, gender, lifestyle, sexual orientation, and age. For example, he would insist that "some clients want contact with the volunteer delivering the meals, others do not. They just want the meal to be placed at the door. Some want to remain removed because they feel guilt and shame, not only for being HIV positive, but also because they are depending on someone else to feed them. We must respect this diversity too."

Jefferson came into our lives in 1993, after being hospitalized for pneumonia. At the time he was living in a single room with a sofa bed and a TV, in a place that was damp and drafty. His unemployment compensation had run out, and he had no money. He was physically and emotionally spent, never left his apartment, and was becoming increasingly depressed.

"I found I had HIV while in an alcohol rehabilitation center," Jefferson reported. "I had been involved in risky sexual behaviors and many of my close friends had died of AIDS. Each death made me more wiped out, which led me to rely more and more upon alcohol. I was caught in a vicious cycle. I kept working until I lost my job as a legislative assistant to a city politician when my boss was beaten in an election. Once all my savings were gone I started selling food stamps to pay the rent. After a year I had nothing left and had to be hospitalized for a long time. I thought I was about to die. I was desolate and lonely and afraid to live. After I got out of the hospital I became a recluse. I felt very guilty about the people I might have infected and started drinking again and using drugs. My family tried to visit me, but I refused to let them see me in that state."

One day a friend came by and brought Jefferson some food. She was a MANNA volunteer and was very concerned about his well-being. She called MANNA, and the next day he began receiving meals. This was how Jefferson recounted his experience.

"When I started receiving MANNA's meals I was so close to the end I thought the angel of death would soon be visiting. When a MANNA volunteer showed up I'd open the door just a crack, grab the meal, and slam it shut fast. One day a MANNA volunteer got to me. It was an elderly lady who had to wear braces on her legs so she could walk. She tried to push the door open just to get in and see me. 'All I want to do is to say the Lord's prayer with you,' she said. I let her in. I was so touched by her that the first couple of times she said the Lord's prayer with me, I wept. Soon I started looking forward to Tuesdays just so I could see her.

"Every week she came, rain, snow, or shine. She never missed a Tuesday. Her braces made it hard for her to walk in the snow, but she'd always arrive glad to see me. I started going downstairs to meet her. I was afraid someone in the neighborhood would hurt her. She was so old and disabled I wanted to protect her.

"I soon became friendly with all the MANNA volunteers. After delivering my meal they would stay and talk. Eventually I got a nicer place, but the volunteers kept coming. Then I broke my leg and the MANNA volunteers were really support-ive. Every day they offered to pick up things from the store, anything I needed. They renewed my faith in humanity. They were so willing to help.

"The food was excellent. At the beginning there were a lot of things I didn't eat. I grew up in a meat and potato home, but MANNA made food in ways I had never been exposed to. I wasn't used to anything exotic. That took some adjustment. I felt that some of the food was not being prepared with African Americans in mind. I called them and told them this. Next week they sent me collard greens and oven-fried chicken. MANNA has made a big difference in my life. I had been eating poorly, but the MANNA meals helped me put back a lot of the weight I had lost and to regain my health.

"Once I had some people staying with me who were homeless and HIV positive. They were not part of any case management system and just stared at me while I ate my MANNA meal. I felt guilty. So I called MANNA and asked for food for them too. The next day they began delivering meals to all of us, no questions asked.

"During one awful snowstorm, some of the volunteers were not able to deliver the meals. MANNA called each day to make sure I was okay. I know that if I had told them I didn't have any food they would have got something to me somehow. If I was not home someone always called me back just to check and see if everything was okay and if I needed anything.

"I don't know where I would be without MANNA. Those people do what they do because it comes from the heart. It's not like it is the 'chic' thing to do. Those volunteers give a lot of time. When you ask them why they volunteer at MANNA they all have a moving story to tell you. Some do it because of a brother or a friend or a son or a child who died of AIDS.

It's their way of working out their sorrow. Or they just want to give back to others all the help they received at some point when they were needy. These stories are what make this organization so spiritual in nature. Everyone who works and volunteers at MANNA has a story that they are silently working through.

"After a while I started working out my life story in a new way. I too became a volunteer, helping those who are living with HIV. This taught me to rethink my own outlook on life. I had been a spiritually focused person growing up, but then I lost it. Before I was diagnosed and my friends started dying, I even questioned the existence of God. But now I have gained a new sense of hope. I now share MANNA's faith in the human spirit.

"In this world dealing with racial and cultural diversity is never easy," Jefferson reminded us. "Considering that MANNA came from a predominantly white church we had to work hard to increase our volunteer base, racially. When MANNA began, most of the clients were gay white men living in the downtown area. That changed very quickly. Now the majority of clients are black and live in really poor neighborhoods. While most of the volunteers who delivered meals to me were white, that didn't bother me, but it upset some people and so I kept this constantly on the MANNA agenda. Today we have volunteers of all races and creeds."

One evening we were sitting around saying farewell to a tireless MANNA worker who was moving on. Some of us spontaneously started talking about the impact MANNA had on our lives. I still get teary eyed when I think of what Jefferson said that night.

"I have been involved in a lot of projects during my life, and I have not seen anything like MANNA before," Jefferson reported. "We never lose sight of our mission — to feed people who have AIDS. We strive not only to nourish them with food, but also to feed the soul and spirit as well. It amazes me when I come to MANNA and see all these people who don't know each other, standing side by side preparing meals for people they don't know. People from all walks of life rub shoulders and work toward a common purpose. It doesn't matter if you are a corporate CEO, a housewife, a plumber. People come together because there is a common denominator at MANNA that all of us share regardless of status. People reach out to learn about and from each other. There is nothing at MANNA that promotes self-interest. Everything is done for someone else.

"When we have board meetings there are no arguments, just debates about how best to fulfill our mission. That's it, nothing more, nothing less. I am sick of AIDS politics, especially when I have to deal with certain government offices. However, I serve on the boards of both MANNA and ActionAIDS and I enjoy this a lot. I have never had to seclude myself because of a conflict. At times I serve as a go-between, and I like being in that position. I'm a client of both organizations and know I have a lot to contribute to each of them. My interest is client-based and that's always how I look at the situation.

"Although HIV has been so divisive it has also created many strong and worthwhile bonds among people. I was recently a part of an executive search committee for Action-AIDS. The committee was made up of seven of the most diverse people you could imagine. On the surface, we had nothing in common. Yet we got along beautifully. That is the one positive side of this disease; it gives me hope. It is so encouraging to see the white gay community still raising hundreds of thousands of dollars even though the disease is not as predominant in that community as it once was. But they haven't let go of the fight.

"It is strange. This disease that threatened to take my life away also gave birth to MANNA, which in turn has helped keep me alive, and to make me feel alive. So many positive things have come into my life as a result of this virus.

I don't take anything for granted anymore, and I appreciate the simple things. Sometimes I do too much because I think my time is limited, but when it brings something positive to another's life, I think it's worth it.

"This disease can still take a big toll on my emotions. I have to ignore others' perceptions and constantly deal with my own guilt about AIDS. I've had to learn that I have nothing to hide. I am now open about everything in my life. HIV is part of my everyday existence. People need to realize how easily this could be their life too. When I say this, people just stare at me. I think attitudes are changing and people are becoming more understanding, especially in the African American community. The black community initially behaved as if HIV didn't affect us, so our black leaders, especially the clergy, felt it was not a priority. This is changing, but we still have a long way to go.

"One year I was feeling very low. It was my birthday. When I opened the door to welcome the MANNA volunteer, there was a lady standing with a cake in her hand singing "Happy Birthday." I hadn't told anyone, but they knew and remembered. At Christmas time I received cards and gifts from elementary school kids. On Thanksgiving, they gave me enough food to have several friends over for dinner. MANNA's service is just filled with a lot of love and has helped me get on with my life. And it all began when, through the blinds on my living room window, I watched a little old lady with braces on her legs who could hardly walk inch her way up my sidewalk in the midst of a blizzard simply to bring me food from MANNA! She was the angel of life."

Social Class in the Pre-manna Days

The biblical account said little about how the Israelites interacted with each other as their food supply shrank. We know they were angry with Moses and God and that Moses was upset because his followers kept deviating from the course God set for them. We also know their will to survive was strong. For clues about what happened in that wilderness we can look at recent events in Northern Ireland or Burma. Throughout all of history, societies facing shortages have divided themselves into "haves" and "have nots," with one level acting like lords while the deprived complain about the inequities. The self-evident truth that all are born equal vanishes when there is a major scarcity of food.

The Israelites knew this in their bones. They had just left a political system where their enslavement provided the Egyptians with the good life. They knew what it was like to be subjugated and deprived while those they served had more than enough. As they left for the promised land, their dream had to be of a place with no division into "haves" and "have nots" because in this new world there would be plenty for everyone.

Imagine their despair as their own community began replicating the one they had escaped. Who gets to eat first is probably the biggest decision made on any day when there is not enough food for all. Take that conflict to the extreme and it becomes who will survive and who will die so that others can live. At that point "women and children first" is but a Hollywood slogan and "Lord of the Flies" becomes reality. Were the Israelites just one step shy of disputes like this? Was this what the Lord was saving them from with manna's dawn?

In an era of barbarism the dog-eat-dog principle rules. There is no established hierarchy about who will "have" and who will "have not." Pecking orders are worked out on the spot depending on who has the upper hand. With the advent of so-called civilization, however, an institution labeled social class emerges. This removes the daily struggle over who eats and who goes without: the uppers always eat; the lowers always lose their rights to food if there are shortages; the ones in between work to sustain this system.[20]

The labor of the lowers props up the infrastructure, which makes it possible for privilege to be perpetuated. Hence the uppers are dependent on them. If there are not enough low-ers, rather than resort to internal barbarism, the trend for ages was to force others into the new lower class. Barbarism was acceptable if it maintained an air of civility. And who were deemed as acceptable pawns in this game? Those with a different religion, a different skin color, a different culture, a different political system. Across the centuries anti-Semitism, racism, colonialism, ethnocentrism, imperialism emerged as ways to prop up the class or caste system.

The children of Israel knew the power of social class. They had been on the wrong end of it for too long. For them the promised land would be unpromising if such a class structure were perpetuated. The new would be no better than the old, and the anguish they went through to start over again would not have been worth it. If getting to civility meant a long sojourn once more in barbarism, this time of their own making instead of one imposed by their former owners, who needed it! And so they asked, "What good is it to be free if we die of starvation or kill ourselves fighting over who will eat? At least while enslaved we were fed."

In every era one of the greatest challenges has been how to deal with the problems of social class and the islands of wealth surrounded by seas of poverty. Marx and Lenin preached about the evils of classism, yet the communists' attempts to build a new social order free of classism's scourge failed. In the so-called "ethnic cleansing" in the Balkans, in the Russian at-tempts to dominate the Chechens, in the Chinese occupation of Tibet we see that these progeny of social class are far from dead. Meanwhile, capitalists continue to accept that social class is part of the natural order, even as they espouse rheto-ric about their efforts to fight against the scourges of racism, sexism, ageism, and all their cousins.

One tenet of civilization is "loyalty to your own people."

Who can argue with that, except when being patriotic means having to hate some designated enemy! I learned an important lesson in this regard in my own family when the U.S. media was focused on a young Cuban boy, Elian Gonzalez, whose divided family was fighting over whether the U.S. should give him political asylum so he could escape "the awful life he would be forced to live in Castro's Cuba," the land of our supposed enemies. My son Phillip had just come back from visiting Cuba with the Philadelphia Boys Choir. When these young ambassadors of song returned the first thing he said was, "Dad, I want to move to Cuba to live." I thought this was his eleven-year-old way of saying he'd had a good time. But he had a more serious message to convey. He had been to the land of the enemy and came home wanting to live in their midst. "Dad," he said, "the Cubans are so very poor — but they're really happy!" A lad could graduate from Yale or earn an Oxford Ph.D. and not make a discovery as meaningful as this. "One can be really poor *and* be really happy — wealth is no passport to joy!"

Like in the original Exodus story, at MANNA we found that in the face of a plague none are immune, that social standing does not protect one from locusts, boils, flies, or HIV, and that all are equally precious in the eyes of the One providing the manna.

The wilderness teaches us that social class is irrelevant in the spiritual scheme of things.

Ten

DEATH'S DAWNING

Lesson 10:
The miraculous was contained
within the mundane.

THE SCRIPTURE TELLS US the wanderers in the wilderness saw the glory of the Lord in the clouds (Exod. 16:10). That's curious to me. When the dawn brings another cloudy day my heart does not jump for joy. I don't celebrate the dankness nor the darkness created by hovering clouds. Nor do I feel exalted by the fierce storm lurking on the horizon. When the outside is leaden and murky, I prefer to snuggle up beside a warm fire. I elect to wait indoors until the tempest has passed. There have also been times when I was enveloped by clouds of despair, the result of either external events or the amorphous disquiets emerging uninvited from my depths. I have "looked to the hills, from whence cometh my help" but never "to the clouds which bringeth respite to my soul."

When asked to paint a picture of God's presence in every-day life, a sun or moon spontaneously appears on my pad. I sense the Divine in the wispy streaks giving a sunset its beauty or the darkness kissing the earth and framing the sun's descent into nightfall. But I don't think of clouds as a place to find God. Nor would I go to a barren wilderness. The rain forest, the high alps, the pounding ocean on unwalked beaches, all filled with images of nature's vitality, draw my soaring spirit. So, when the Israelites looked toward the *wilderness* and saw the glory of the Lord appearing in a *cloud*, for me the imagery is filled with contradictions.

While tradition has labeled the four decades between the Red Sea and the River Jordan as the wilderness period, in reality the Israelites were perpetually in a metaphorical wilderness. Their 430 years as slaves in Egypt and the military battles by which they took Canaan from its occupants were wildernesses of another kind. The promised milk and honey did not come easily, and it must have been devastating to discover that when they ate the produce of the new land the manna ceased. They gained their own turf and food but lost the daily reminder of God's presence, the falling grace raining down from heaven upon their undernourishment. Such irony, from slavery into militarism, from manna into consumerism, one wilderness swapped for another.

Yet the reality was that much of God's revelation came to the deprived in the wilderness years, not to the resourced in the good times. The Israelites became the chosen people in the wilderness. They also internalized each other's experiences of God. Hence, when Joshua was asked to take off his sandals because the place where he stood was deemed to be holy ground, he did so spontaneously, for Moses' vision of the bush that burned without being consumed was branded upon his heart. "This piece of dirt beneath your feet is sacred land" was a motif that grew until all that stretched before them became the holy land.

Thanks to MANNA, AIDS became my wilderness, and Jesse, a homeless African American man with HIV, became my cloud containing God.

Letting Go of Protective Boundaries

We learned that volunteering at MANNA involved us all in things we did not expect and that it was useful to place clear boundaries around our engagement. Hence we gave a clear message to volunteers: "While you are here give your all, but when your work is done return to your homes and your community and get on with the other parts of your life." This was a fine organizational posture to take, but as the stories conveyed in this book attest, the heart does not fit into neatly defined compartments. When a person with HIV touched us, our connection to that person did not end when we took off our apron or parked the car after making our allocated meal deliveries. When we recognized this, we suggested that each volunteer and each client define whatever relationship they wanted beyond the formal limits of MANNA. Some, like Glen and Charles, built lifelong ties. Others had encounters lasting only a few seconds. Some carried each other in their hearts all day. Others worked at a distance and had no face-to-face contact with those they served.

One thing happened to me I never expected. Perhaps had I understood better what we were getting into I might have anticipated it. But it grew imperceptibly until one day it was a reality I both appreciated and felt burdened by. I had asked so many of our neighbors to help with MANNA that I became known as "the teacher on the corner who helps people with AIDS." So it was not unusual for Sara or me to answer our doorbell and find a stranger saying, "I have AIDS. Can you please help me with . . . ?"

This would not have occurred everywhere in the city. We live in West Philadelphia in a pleasant neighborhood intermeshed with extreme poverty. For us this is home. But we daily encounter people with no place to sleep and for whom feeling at home in their bodies, in their relationships, in their environment is but a distant dream. They regularly knock on our door asking for handouts or seeking some kind of contact. Living in such a neighborhood brings little physical risk but a large emotional one: it is easy to grow hardened to the vulnerabilities of others and close off the raw parts of ourselves that can be nourished only when left exposed.

A couple of years after MANNA began I realized I had become vulnerable in a new way: how was I going to stop AIDS from consuming my every waking hour? How was I going to place personal boundaries around my engagement so that I had the reserves to do my job, bathe my kids, walk the dog? How was I going to remain open to the pain of people on the street asking strangers for help?

Fortunately, Jesse, a homeless man who regularly dropped by our home, taught me several critical lessons. He helped me see that many people with AIDS would not interact with MANNA because they feared the institutionalizing effect of receiving help from such organizations. Only by having a personal relationship with people who worked there would they freely accept the gift of food. He also showed me that by walking arm in arm with those embroiled in deep suffering I too would find a balm for my aching heart.

A Surprising Spiritual Guide

Although he never intended it to be this way, Jesse, who had barged into my life uninvited, became my spiritual guide. Our relationship began in the cold and looked like it would end on a bone-chilling night, but the glow that radiated from the soul of this African American man could not be extinguished by the sleet and biting winds of winter.

More than a decade ago, when our twins were toddlers, a rap at the back door summoned us from our evening meal. We were used to callers ringing the front door bell, an adolescent wanting $5 to shovel the fresh snow on the sidewalk, a volunteer seeking support for Greenpeace, a child selling Girl Scout cookies. We welcomed petitioners but felt overtaxed by them. Their causes were always noble, but they came during last-minute dinner preparations, or as the children were being bathed, or in the midst of bedtime stories.

No one had ever come to the back door before. Sara responded to his impatient knock. It was Jesse, a man in his forties with a sweet face and a charming manner. He was asking for work and payment with "anything you can spare to help feed my daughter and my wife." That was unusual. Most homeless men in our neighborhood ask for money for themselves, not their family. Sara and Jesse fell into a lengthy conversation. Sensing his kind heart, Sara went to the larder, gave him a few things, and asked him to return the next day to wash our family car. That night he entered our lives in a way no homeless person had ever done before. Over the next few months he was a regular. Then suddenly he stopped visiting. We wondered what had happened. Slowly Jesse faded from our thoughts.

Four years later he reappeared at our front door. He had been in the South working on an uncle's farm. For a while his family was fine, but things had fallen apart. His wife had struggled with a serious drug problem, but only on becoming a Muslim did things change for her. Her conversion led her to a drug-free life and a sense of inner stability she had long craved. This destabilized their marriage. As she improved, their relationship disintegrated. Eventually they separated.

Losing his wife and his daughter, Lyn, threw Jesse into a deep depression. For a period, his despair was so intense he could not connect with anyone. For several years Jesse had no contact with them. He worked on his uncle's farm in South Carolina for a while, but after a fight he headed north and ended up back in Philadelphia. He got a job and a small place but could not hang on to either. Once more he fell into the cycle of homelessness.

We were happy to see Jesse again, and once more he helped with weekend chores. Conversation was sparse, but as we shoveled snow and raked leaves together, we got to know him well. Jesse had a good heart, a generous spirit, and a solid work ethic. Slowly he let us see his pain. He was still in love with his wife, and he teared up when he spoke about missing his daughter. He felt like a failure as a father and blamed himself for not being a good provider.

Jesse had a hard time keeping a job. Whenever he got steady work something went wrong. Once, working as a parking attendant, he just missed being caught in the gunfire of two assailants. He quit on the spot. Another time he got fired for not calling in when he was sick. He did not have a phone and was so ill it was hard to get down the stairs in the derelict building where he had a room. The pay phone on the corner had been vandalized. He tried to walk five blocks to the next coin-operated phone but halfway there gave up, dragged himself back to bed, and collapsed. The next day, still sick, he went to work but was laid off. Then he became a roofer's assistant, hurt his back, and could not continue.

From then on Jesse eked out an existence sweeping sidewalks. Usually he earned enough to rent a room and feed himself. The rest of the time he slept on the streets or crashed on his cousin's couch. He was entitled to $200 a month from the government but only got one check in three because he failed to let the authorities know his whereabouts. He could never hold on to money though. If he had a few extra dollars he gave them to someone more needy than he was.

One evening he was waiting on my front step as I arrived home. He could hardly contain his excitement. "My daughter and her mom are back in Philadelphia," he blurted out. I had never seen Jesse joyous. His skinny frame no longer had the gait of a defeated man, and his face, wrinkled by decades of extreme hardship, was filled with delight. Jesse did not expect to be reconciled with his wife, but seeing Lyn, his thirteen-year-old daughter, excited him. He had prayed to be reunited with her. This time he was determined to succeed as a father. In the hours since meeting them, Jesse had found a place with a second room so Lyn could stay with him. For the next few weeks there was a spring in his step. Becoming a father again offered a little of the healing his spirit had cried out for.

Within weeks all was not well. Lyn's mother was ill and could not cope. Jesse was not privy to the problems. He suspected cancer. She had to be hospitalized, and for several weeks the full burden of parenting fell on him. Jesse wanted to do well by Lyn. Most days he was at our house seeking extra work so he could buy her new shoes or a dress, or pressing us for advice about how to be her advocate at school. We helped when we could, but became nervous about the intensity of his dependency upon us. It seemed that every time he had a need he was asking for our help.

Then came the news. Lyn's mother had died in the early hours of the morning. This death provoked many emotions in Jesse. He was sad that his daughter had lost her mother. He ached for Lyn, who was torn apart by grief and was pained by his inability to take away her anguish. Yet he was happy because Lyn would be with him full time. Such irony. Death had snatched away her mother and given her father new life. This lifted Jesse out of his own plight and plunged him into the darkness enveloping Lyn. Despite the joy created by her return, Lyn's pain was added to his own, leaving him to carry twice as much hurt in his heart.

A Devastating Loss

The next few weeks raced by for Jesse. His happiness was tempered by his economic reality. Even earning enough to take Lyn to a movie was a burden. His big dilemma though was how to provide for her safety. The only place he could afford was located in the roughest part of the city. He tried to be there when Lyn returned from school, but that was hard given his habit of looking for work at all hours of the day. One night, near where they lived, Jesse was mugged and lost all the food money he had earned. Within an hour he was ringing our bell asking if we could help him out. There have been only a few times I've happily handed over all the cash we had in the house. That was one of them.

Three months into his new life of fathering Jesse concluded he had to make some moves. He felt he could not keep Lyn safe in Philadelphia and decided to return to the rural South. With the arrival of spring and the end of school in sight a sense of urgency came upon him. He called his cousin Jan, who lived in South Carolina, and arranged for Lyn to stay with her and her husband for a few weeks until he could make a permanent move. Lyn was distraught by Jesse's decision. She was thankful Jan was willing to take her in but was adamant that she wanted to stay close to her dad. She was still dealing with the loss of her mom and did not want to be separated from him too. Jesse assured her it would only be for a few weeks, but she didn't believe him. Off they went to South Carolina. He stayed for a week. She pleaded with him not to leave. Jesse was moved by her protests but brushed them aside and returned to Philadelphia. He was convinced she would be safer in the rural South than in the urban North and felt his highest priority had to be keeping her out of harm's way.

Early the next day Jesse was at our front door as our house-hold stirred. He had traveled all night from South Carolina and was hoping for as much work as possible that day so he could save up for his permanent move to be reunited with Lyn. I could not fathom why Jesse had come back. This city offered him little. He had no job or a special place he called home. I tried to talk him into gathering his things and getting on the bus so he could rejoin Lyn right away. He listened, nodded, and mumbled, "I'll go as soon as I can."

That day he labored hard for ten hours, doing many odd jobs in our neighborhood and earning $80. By 6:00 p.m. he was exhausted and went back to his small apartment. Tacked to his door, on a piece of scrap paper scribbled by a roomer in this rundown building, was the following message. "Jan called. This afternoon Lyn was walking along the riverbank. She slipped, fell in, and drowned."

No words can describe the despair that descended on Jesse. That night he sat in our living room for hours, first wailing uncontrollably and then sobbing quietly until he was spent. Jesse's melancholy knew no bounds. He repeated over and over things like, "Why would God do this to me! Why didn't I teach her how to swim!" At midnight he was on the bus again heading back to pick up Lyn's body for burial in Philadelphia. My heart had never ached for another person as it did that evening. Jesse's anguish was my anguish. Across recent days Lyn had become his main reason for living. With her gone he wanted it all to end. He'd have been happiest if he had died that night.

During the many hours he spent with us that evening, as we looked into his face both Sara and I saw, for a sustained period, an expression we had never witnessed before. It was as if his emotional rawness had exposed a part of the human spirit normally kept hidden. In his wounds we had seen the purest and kindest heart imaginable. Sara captured it perfectly: "I think I just saw the face of God." There, in the thoroughly broken heart of a man, the presence of the Almighty was evident. Both of us felt awed as we were ushered into a new form of understanding that night.

Three days later Jesse returned with Lyn's body. We saw him every few hours that week. Apart from trying to grasp that his daughter was actually gone, he was preoccupied with buying Lyn a new dress for her interment. With sadness he lamented, "Not only did I fail to keep my daughter safe, I can't even buy a new dress to bury her in." It was critical to him that he actually buy special clothes for Lyn and to pay for them himself. However, there was no time for him to earn any money before her funeral. This was something he, as a father, had to do for her. Eventually he settled for borrowing $100, so long as I let him pay it off.

Another thing was troubling him. He didn't believe the story about Lyn's death. His cousin had told the police that a group of kids had been playing together on the embankment and Lyn had slipped. None of the children knew how to swim, and no one tried to rescue her. By the time they got help it was too late. Jesse was sure this was a lie. He had talked with these kids, and they told him a story that matched perfectly Jan's account. But they were devoid of emotion. He knew that children who witnessed such a trauma would be more distressed, more expressive, more regretful. He was sure they were not even present when Lyn drowned and had been coached to tell this tale to cover up some awful truth.

Jesse thought Jan was responsible. He suspected she was present when Lyn drowned and might even have caused it. Jesse's distress was so severe it was easy to suspect his mind was playing tricks on him. Perhaps his unconscious was trying to find someone to blame. But I knew Jesse well enough to sense he was on to something but could not imagine what it might be.

Two days after the burial Jesse was called by the district attorney in South Carolina to tell him about a court hearing that was certain to rule that this death was not accidental. Jesse was almost out of control. He was convinced that Jan was responsible for Lyn's death, and he wanted revenge. He hoped Jan would see out her days in prison. The rage was useful for Jesse in the short run, because it gave him an external outlet for the anger he had been turning in on himself. Once more he set off for the South. But, when he was halfway there, he got off the bus and headed back north. He saw that his anger was a total displacement. "There's nothing I can do to bring Lyn back. It doesn't matter any more how she died," he said on his return. "She's gone. If Jan did it, God will deal with her, not me. I can't be the judge." Jesse's turning around helped him find his inner core again. This was how he expressed it. "I was ready to blame anyone but me. But my

anger made me as bad as them. I must stop this. I've gotta
preserve the tiny bit of dignity I have left."

As he said this I was amazed that he had actually managed
to purge himself of the vindictiveness that I suspect would rule
my life until my final breath were I in his situation. Jesse's pain
was overwhelmingly visible, but it was matched by the clarity
and purity of his heart. I thought of another's words at another
time: "Forgive them for they know not what they do."

A week later Jesse received a call from Jan's husband. She
had confessed all. This was the story. Jan was an alcoholic who
liked to go fishing in a boat so she could hide while drinking.
That day she had taken Lyn with her. By midafternoon Jan
was drunk. She asked Lyn to hand her another beer from
the cooler. Lyn refused. She was frightened by Jan's aggres-
sion, which had increased as she got more drunk. Lyn, who
had seen drugs destroy her own mother, refused to hand over
a beer. Jan, who was considerably overweight, stood up and
destabilized the boat. She belligerently pushed Lyn aside to
get another drink, and as she did so Lyn was thrown over-
board. Jan was too intoxicated to help. She could not swim
and was too afraid to attempt any rescue. After a while she
went to the shore and convinced some children to tell their
lie about how Lyn had died.

Jesse was relieved to know the truth. It confirmed his earlier
suspicions. He decided to keep away from the courts as they
dealt with Jan. He was carrying too much blame himself to get
into her guilt. He doubted he would ever recover from these
wounds but resolved to work hard, stabilize his own life, and
try to live as fulfilling an existence as he could. "Lyn would
have wanted that," he concluded.

We saw a lot of Jesse that summer. He gave up the two
rooms he had shared with Lyn. He could not stand the memories. After a couple of weeks of being homeless he moved in
with a cousin, a man whose wife was addicted to crack and
who was never around. Jesse's cousin had three young kids

and was fathering them alone. Being around the children was therapeutic for Jesse.

Since Lyn's death Jesse had not got more than an hour or two of sleep a night. Nor could he digest any food. So over the weeks he began to look very drawn and older than his years. He was naturally thin and had no spare weight to lose. He got the flu, which lingered far too long. Despite these setbacks his spirit was good. He actually came to feel vital again and dared to hope for a little brightness in his future.

We went away on our family vacation and for a few weeks left behind the cares of our lives in Philadelphia. During that time, though, Sara and I often wondered aloud how Jesse was doing. We did not have to wait long to find out.

Startling News

We had not been in the house more than an hour upon our re-turn before Jesse was there. He was beside himself. His cousin had thrown him out of his house and everything looked bleak. "I can't make a go of it here any more," he said. "Older black men used to get respect. Now we get abused every day. I am going down South. My uncle wants me to work on his farm. I'm leaving tonight. I waited to say goodbye to you. You've been my family. I had to see you before I went. I gotta thank you for all you've done."

Sara and I were stunned by his decision. Something did not ring true about his explanation. He was leaving that night, never to return! Then he looked at me and almost demanded that I drive him to the bus station and give him the money for his fare. I was willing to do both, but this was out of character for Jesse, and I wondered what was really up.

But Jesse was adamant. He and Sara said their tear-filled goodbyes. As Jesse and I got in the car for the twenty–block drive to bus station, he let the next bomb fall. "I didn't want to tell you this in the house. I couldn't face Sara. Please tell her for me. While you were away I was very sick. I could not keep down any food. They put me in the hospital. They found out I've got AIDS. That explains why my cough wouldn't go away, why I can't eat, and why I've lost so much weight."

At that moment I wanted to take him back to my home, to settle him in for a few nights, to take care of him. He was in no shape to travel. He was frightened and overwhelmed beyond comprehension.

"I now know why my wife came back to Philadelphia. She knew she had AIDS and was dying and wanted to get me reconnected to Lyn before she was gone."

"Did she tell you she had AIDS?"

"No, but it all adds up now. Several years ago she was doing drugs a lot and was with the worst crowd. They were using each other's needles. They didn't know anything about HIV back then and no one cared anyway."

"How long have you had the virus?" I asked.

"At least six years. That's the last time I had sex with her. It's the last time I had sex with anyone. I've never done drugs or been with men."

Sitting at the bus station I pleaded with Jesse to remain in Philadelphia a few more days. I knew all the services available to people living with AIDS in this city and invited him to stay in our home. But he was determined to leave that night. He expected to die soon and wanted to be with his uncle for his final few weeks. So that night we said farewell to each other.

He boarded the bus and we waved our goodbyes. I asked him to call me or to write me or have his uncle contact me, but there was never any news. Once more he was gone from our lives.

Months later I learned that he never made it to his uncle's farm. He had not even reached Washington, D.C., before he had an extreme anxiety attack. The driver, thinking he was having a psychotic episode, stopped the bus and called for an ambulance, which took him to the nearest Veterans Administration hospital. Jesse remained in that VA for six months, during which time he received his first treatment for his HIV infection.

Since we had heard nothing for so long I had concluded that Jesse had made it to the South and died. I knew this was what he wanted. He imagined that death would reunite him with Lyn, maybe even his former wife, and end the anguish of his earthly existence. That summer, however, while we were on vacation a person house-sitting for us called to say that Jesse had returned, was well, and was asking for us. I was stunned and looked forward to seeing him again.

The next year Jesse and I did many things together. Mostly I was happy to have him around, but there were two things that were extremely distressing to me.

First, when he dropped by he expected me to respond immediately to his needs. He sometimes felt like another son, and I was troubled by the things I did that reinforced his dependency. I tried to talk with him about it, but Jesse got upset and said, "I apologize for bothering you." "Please understand, Jesse, I am not bothered that you come around, but sometimes I can't drop everything and respond to you exactly the way you want and when you want it."

The second thing that troubled me, and this was far worse, was having to watch the day-to-day effect AIDS was having on him. HIV is merciless, and I hated being a witness to its brutal effects. To sit in my yard with Jesse as he coughed up blood, to watch him deal with the embarrassment of a bowel movement that struck unexpectedly as we raked leaves together, to see him unable to recognize me on the street until I called to him because his eyesight was fading, were not things to which I was easily reconciled, despite my years of involvement with MANNA. Every new occasion was as shocking for me as the first time. Yet despite this I wanted to be with Jesse through his decline. I was inspired by his courage, yet nights like the following were very difficult.

It was 10:30 p.m. There was an impatient ring of the doorbell. I knew who it was. This was the third evening in a row Jesse had come by. I wanted to ignore it, but that was impossible. Within seconds he would press it again, activating five gongs instead of three, then eight. Jesse's actions at our front door were distinctive. No one else ever held the button for so long or gave us so little time to respond before pressing it again.

I was exhausted. The children had been slow getting to bed, and I was anxious lest the stomach bug that had kept one of the boys up most of the previous night had been passed on to another child. Six attacks of nausea and three new sets of sheets in one night had done me in. We were all sleep-deprived. I hadn't even asked Sara how many times she'd been up during that evening.

Half an hour earlier I had slumped into my favorite chair, ready to unwind from the burdens of my day. I had turned on the TV to check the sports scores. Jesse's ringing had woken me from my catnap, an art form I have perfected sitting in front of the tube.

"Jesse, how are you doing?" It was a perfunctory greeting.

"I've got three dollars and need another $1.50 to buy some Pampers. Take it off the money you give me for my Saturday work."

"You having trouble with your bowels again?"

"Yep."

It was so hard. Monday night Jesse had asked for $4.00 to buy kerosene to warm his freezing place. Tuesday it was $3.00 for a sandwich. This night it was to help him buy diapers. Who knew what the next night might bring. It wasn't the money. The hardship was looking so regularly into the face of AIDS, seeing the brutal assault of this virus on a person's dignity, having it on my doorstep every day tugging fiercely at my heart. For it to be Jesse was particularly difficult, given all he had gone through.

Jesse needed a great deal of help, but he had grown weary of established organizations. He refused to call MANNA or any of the other AIDS agencies in Philadelphia to access their services. He felt embarrassed when they asked for his phone number and he had to say that not only did he have no phone, but he had no stable address either. He was also hanging tenaciously to every vestige of independence he could retain.

I was eager for Jesse to get MANNA meals. He desperately needed them because the wasting syndrome was fast overtaking him. But he refused to become a regular MANNA client. Only when I personally went to pick up a MANNA meal and took it to him myself was Jesse willing to avail himself of our wonderful and life-sustaining food. Ultimately I realized that for MANNA to reach people like him we had to live in intense, day-to-day, mutual relationship with them. This confronted me with the harsh reality that MANNA's distribution systems failed to reach the people who had grown disillusioned by the bulk of our institutions.

Jesse showed me that there were many people needing MANNA who could only be reached by volunteers willing to hang out under the bridges or in the many cracks and crevices of this vast city. He was teaching me about a task MANNA's leadership had yet to confront.

As the summer months turned to fall and the cold visited our city streets, I suspected Jesse would not see out the year. His tall, thin frame already had no flesh left on it. Food no longer sustained him, and every few days he seemed to catch another flu. He was in and out of the VA hospital every couple of weeks. His physician told him it would not be long.

A Final Goodbye

It was a bitter January. Jesse was still in rapid decline, but death was slow to arrive. However, another event had taken over our lives. In the days immediately following her visit that

Christmas Sara's mother discovered she had colon cancer and needed major surgery. This brought many new stresses. Then it was discovered her cancer had spread to the liver and that she had only a few months to live. Sara's dad had died twenty years earlier, and the care for her mom, who had walked with crutches all her adult life due to polio, would fall on Sara and her siblings.

The very night that Sara, who was away in Rochester, learned that her mom's cancer was terminal, Jesse visited to tell me that his doctor thought he would die before the week was over.

This was an overwhelming day for all of us. I was busy trying to get ready to take the children to Rochester to visit grandma in the hospital. We needed to be together as a family since it was going to be a while before Sara would be back in Philadelphia.

It was obvious the end was close for Jesse. He could hardly walk any more, was almost blind, and was coughing up blood every few minutes. We talked at length about his anticipation of dying and how his faith was sustaining him. He believed he would soon be with his daughter and grandmother, a Cherokee Indian, with whom he was very identified. A deeply spiritual woman, she had planted in Jesse an appreciation for the Almighty that had grown stronger over years. He was convinced that death would bring a reunion with his grandmother, the one person from his childhood who had loved him unconditionally. When he had first told me about her I was pleased because she was one of the few figures in his family circle who did not seem tragic.

Jesse's mother had died when he was five as a result of family violence. She was in the kitchen preparing a meal when Jesse's dad returned home in a drunken stupor. Something she did enraged him. He grabbed her and threw her against the wall. She slipped, banged her head hard on the stove, and slumped to the floor unconscious. Her father ran from the house. Jesse, who witnessed the scene, called the ambulance. His mom never regained consciousness and died a few days later. That night Jesse lost both his mom and his dad, who disappeared and was never heard from again. In addition he was left with the private burden of knowing what had really happened. His dad was never held accountable for the killing.

Alcohol had deprived Jesse of his mother, his father, and his daughter. Drugs had both destroyed his marriage and been the vehicle by which the HIV virus entered the bodies of his former wife and then him.

My farewell with Jesse that night was very emotional. We both believed he would be gone by the time I returned from Rochester. Being very careful, since Jesse was coughing up a lot of blood, we embraced each other and wept together, both celebrating that our lives had intersected as they had. Coining Sara's phrase, I told Jesse that on two separate occasions I felt I had seen in him the face of God. He nodded weakly and shyly, not saying a word.

He asked me for a final favor. "Would you give me the money to go watch a movie? Then I'll go to the hospital." I gave him $10. I offered to drive him but he wanted to walk.

As I watched Jesse stumble down the block, each labored movement of his feet advancing him only a few inches, I wondered if I should have taken him directly to the hospital myself. However, I was quickly distracted by the demands of the children, a call from Sara about the continuing trauma in Rochester, and the need to pack the car and ready the children for the six-hour drive ahead. Needless to say, during the drive my thoughts vacillated back and forth between Jesse and Sara's mom, punctuated by the needs of two eight-year-olds and one five-year-old.

Once we were in Rochester it was wonderful to be reunited as a whole family and to give the children's grandma the gift of our presence. I told Sara of my teary goodbyes with Jesse, that he sent her his love. For the next two days I was centered mostly on my family and the anxiety of what our lives would be like as we prepared to care for Sara's dying mother.

Monday was spent driving back to Philadelphia with the kids. An hour after our return the doorbell rang. It was Jesse's cousin. She had come to tell me that he had just died. She handed me a farewell note Jesse scratched on a piece of paper. His last request was that she come to tell me when he died. She was exhausted from having sat with him around the clock, but took the time to tell me what his death had been like and mentioned in passing that he had been in room 303.[21]

The next day I called the VA hospital to ask for information about Jesse's burial. I imagined that as a Vietnam Vet his funeral costs would be covered and thought the military might have some protocol for dealing with his body. I wanted to know what was to happen. To my dismay, they told me an unbelievable story. They assured me that no AIDS patient had died over the last few days, that there was no one, nor had there ever been anyone, by Jesse's name treated for AIDS in that particular VA hospital. I even spoke to the nurses on the ward and asked pointedly about the man who had been in room 303 over the weekend. No, Jesse had not been there, and the person occupying that room had not died.

I called all the funeral homes I thought might be pressed into service, but none had heard about Jesse. It was perplexing. I spoke again with Jesse's cousin and grilled her on the story she had told me. She was adamant. Jesse had been in room 303 and had died around 6:00 p.m. on Monday. She knew nothing about funeral arrangements because some family in the South wanted him buried down there.

I was in the midst of a very busy workweek plus I had the added responsibilities of being a single dad. Perhaps if I had the time I might have gone to the VA hospital myself and forced my way onto the AIDS ward and got to the bottom of it. But with each call the picture got more confusing. I was so overtaxed I decided to let it go. I accepted that Jesse was dead, concluded that the VA was giving out disinformation for reasons I would never uncover, and decided that what was to happen to Jesse's body did not ultimately matter. Over the next few days I began grieving for Jesse, talked about his death in my Saturday morning men's group, immersed myself in my MANNA work, and slowly let him slip into the vast numbers of people I, and so many of my MANNA friends, knew who had died of AIDS. Of course for me Jesse would never be a statistic, but the press to deal with those still living held a greater priority.

A few days later Sara returned, and we started preparing for her mother's decline. That week we were also preoccupied with the removal of a large tree, which had dumped a huge portion of its trunk on our roof. It threatened to do more damage and be a safety hazard if we failed to remove it quickly.

Surprised by Life

Early on Saturday morning, twelve days after Jesse's death, I was driving through my neighborhood, thinking about the pile of wood in my yard waiting to be split and stacked, a task Jesse might have helped me with. Suddenly emerging from a building near my home was Jesse. I was sure I was hallucinating. I screeched to a halt, backed my car up, and looked at the spot where I had seen him. He had vanished. I jumped out of my car and suddenly there he was. I called this apparition by name. He turned. I didn't think ghosts could hear. I walked toward him and grabbed him. It was Jesse all right. I was not hallucinating at all. That morning began a rebirthing for me that continues to this day and I imagine will be ongoing until my final breath.

This was the story. Jesse was pronounced dead by the local VA hospital around 6:00 p.m., Monday, February 5, 1996.[22] His body was placed in storage overnight. The next morning he was shaved from head to toe and tagged to be sent off to a local medical school as a cadaver. I guess the VA felt that since he was an indigent and had no family to care about him, they were at liberty to dispose of his body as they liked. However, the person tending him noticed a faint pulse.

Jesse was in a coma for the next six days. When he emerged the doctors ran numerous tests, which showed no evidence of HIV. Despite his previous positive diagnosis and many retests there was no sign of the virus. This surprised Jesse's doctor, who had never seen this kind of turnaround or a case of the HIV virus going underground for a period.

What happened to Jesse in the interim cannot be expressed in words and any attempt to describe it will be but a faint echo of his actual experience. In short, he had a near-death experience, including very reassuring encounters with his daughter and his grandmother, now beings of intense, translucent light in this other world. He described sensations that so transcend what we humans can access we cannot grasp them. Everything radiated light and left Jesse at peace and eager to remain in this new place. He was most upset when it was communicated to him that his time to die had not yet come. He groped for why he was to return to this life but got no answers, just the assurance that this was right for him.

Jesse was quite circumspect about what he was willing to tell me. I sensed he knew a great deal that he was censoring. I asked him if this was right, and he said yes. He told me that on his journey to the other side he had gleaned some insights about me, piquing my curiosity, of course.

To my amazement Jesse told me in significant detail some things about my life growing up in Australia, which we had never discussed. I was curious about how he knew these things, but he refused to say. Then he mentioned encountering our family dog and gave me vivid details, which I had never conveyed to anyone. I asked him explicitly, "You've seen my life unfold, right?" He nodded. "And are you going to tell me about it?" I eagerly asked. He laughed. "Of course not. It is for you to find out as you live it." That was all he would say.

What most amazed me was how he looked. Jesse had put on a lot of weight, seemed ten years younger than I had ever seen him, and had regained his strength. Only two weeks earlier, he was less than a hundred pounds, could hardly walk, was coughing up blood and was so short of breath he had to sit every few minutes. This Saturday he was as strong as an ox and helped me split, cart, and pile more than a cord of wood. We worked side by side for several hours cleaning up the tree that had come down in our yard. He easily matched my energies. Several times I asked him to stop, not to overreach, but he was adamant that he was up for it. He was right. At no point over the next several weeks did his heightened physical energies decrease.

At the end of that day all my assumptions about what con-stituted life and death had been blown away. How could one be that sick, be declared dead, be on the verge of becoming a specimen in a medical student's anatomy class, and come out of a coma as well as Jesse did? Something quite miraculous had occurred before my eyes.

For the next several months Jesse remained exceedingly well. However, that HIV virus had not magically disappeared. It had hidden out in some out-of-the-way corner of the body, lurking there in an undetected form for a while. A year later he started showing once more the early symptoms of HIV. My heart sank. Why was Jesse being asked to go through the full cycle a second time? But he took it in stride, viewing it as part of the lessons of life. In a way that transcended words, I had caught a close-up glimpse of what all MANNA clients know: in the worst of times they can be surprised by supreme joy, and in the best of times their dreams can be shattered.

When Jesse went to the other side during his brush with death, he got a glimpse of what was ahead for him. Today he continues to live in this world. He believes his ongoing existence on earth is important for reasons yet to become clear. He is eager to move on, to continue his journey in the next plane. He has seen the angels, he knows his destiny is to be with them, and he is waiting until his time comes.

Conclusion

FROM SCARCITY
TO ABUNDANCE

D URING THE FOUR YEARS since my everyday involvement
with MANNA ended I have wondered if there is a
simple way to summarize all that we learned. The answer is
yes. It goes as follows: *the natural order is predicated on the
principle of abundance while scarcity is a psychological condition
expressing our existential angst; the gift of manna is an invitation
to take the spiritual journey from scarcity to abundance.* I conclude with a few thoughts about that path from scarcity to
abundance.

•

*I have a deep wish to talk once again with Ernest Sommerville,
First Presbyterian's beloved pastor for a quarter of a century, who
died unexpectedly soon after he conducted our wedding ceremony.
If I could reach him I'd tell him about MANNA and all that is in
this book. I'd include the following remembrance in my cover note.*

Dear Dr. Sommerville,
It was the mid-1980s. You, who had the capacity to reach
the soul while taking our minds to the farthest horizons, were
leaning over the pulpit in your characteristic style, coming to
the end of a sermon on the feeding of the five thousand. This
Sunday you had moved us across the whole intellectual landscape, inviting us to consider what it meant that a Nazarene

named Jesus, who calmed the tempest, healed the sick, raised
the dead, cast out demons, made the lame to walk, restored
sight to the blind, had taken a few loaves and a couple of fish
and magically multiplied them so there was enough to feed
several thousand people.

You asked us to reflect on why this story was preserved for
posterity. If this event literally occurred, why was it important
to retell? Was it providing further evidence that Jesus was
"the One" Israel had been waiting for since the prophesies
of Isaiah? Or was it telling us that God would provide for
all our physical needs? Or was it like a parable, a story that
conveyed a major message, and if so, what was the point we
were supposed to get?

All four Gospel writers describe this event and highlight
the signature of Jesus. He "*took* the bread, *blessed* it, *broke* it,
and *gave* it to the people." I recently heard Walter Brueggemann discuss this special moment where past and future were
connected: "Manna, the symbol of God's generosity amidst
the scarcity of the wilderness, was linked to the Passover and
to the breaking of bread at the last supper. On the occasion of the final meal eaten with Jesus, the disciples, without
knowing it, were celebrating the fact that abundance vetoed
scarcity."[23]

Most of the details of your sermon from the mid-1980s
have long since faded from memory, but I recall being trans-
fixed by it. The Sunday School me was convinced that this
event really happened and that it was the kind of miracle all
of us could expect whenever we had special physical needs,
be they hunger, illness, or psychosis. The anthropological me
was awed by the capacity of the Jewish and Christian re-
ligions to weave together a rich tapestry of symbols into a
whole belief system that gave meaning to aspects of life that
otherwise seemed senseless. The philosophical me was fully
absorbed in the idea that God was in the business of providing food for the soul and that I should take the manna and

the "bread broken and given for" me as a metaphoric treasure and hold them close to my heart as a perpetual reminder of God's presence and investment in both my physical and spiritual well-being.

All parts of me were feeling well nourished by your sermon and I was ready for your "Amen" signaling the end. Then you offered a provocative thought I never expected. It has stayed with me and was a constant guide during my involvement with MANNA.

"I have one more suggestion about what might have happened that day," you said, leaning close and speaking quietly so we were forced to listen intently to get your point. You then offered a more human version of the hillside feast, by inviting us to imagine that these people who had been following Jesus around, as they had John the Baptist before him, knew the drill pretty well. They realized they'd be out there under the hot sun for hours, eagerly soaking up the words of this latest prophet, and would have packed a picnic lunch. However, many newcomers were probably caught up in the crowd and were likely to be unprepared. Some people had food, you suggested, and some did not. Some were "haves" and some were "have nots." Then a small boy stepped forward and gave Jesus the lunch his mom had packed for him. Jesus blessed this food, and in so doing placed all the people under the blessing. And the hearts of the people were opened and everyone stopped hoarding their picnic lunches and started sharing them with each other. At the end, the disciples gathered up all that had been left uneaten and there were baskets and baskets of leftovers.

"Perhaps Jesus took the seven loaves and two fish and transformed them into enough to feed five thousand. Or perhaps he opened the hearts of the people so they shared what they had with each other. I don't know what really happened," you said. "But I ask you. Which do you think was the greater miracle?"

Ernest, I now understand what that sermon meant. Thank you. I also feel confident that as you read this letter and this book you will simply smile and give a gentle, knowing nod.

•

The current world population is six billion people. That's a lot of mouths to feed. However, even using current agricultural methods, there is plenty of food for all. In fact, without any technological advances in food production, we have the ability to feed twelve billion. The miracle of food production has already occurred, and the science required to continue these advances through several more stages has also been placed in the hands of humanity. Yet today there are millions and millions of people who are starving. How can this be? And how is it that we have been unable to overcome the scourge of malnutrition, especially in the poorest nations of the world?

The problem, of course, is not the lack of food but a set of political systems that have made it impossible for an effective, efficient, and wholesome food distribution system to be developed. It's as if our collective hearts have never been opened to the vision of all people on earth being entitled to the manna, whether or not they can personally afford it within the social, political, and economic system we humans have constructed.

Food scarcity is not part of the natural order of things. It is a product of the choices made by human beings. And if it was constructed by humans surely it can be altered by humans. But what would it take? I'd like to suggest that it will require our shifting from a paradigm of scarcity to one of abundance.

That will not be easy, but the path is clear. As with similar programs in other cities like "Project Open Hand" in San Francisco and "God's Love We Deliver" in New York, the miracle of MANNA was that the hearts of so many of us once closed to people living with AIDS were opened wide. When we collectively stopped operating on the scarcity principle and started sharing our communal abundance, with food and hearts woven together, we discovered that everything freely given away was returned, magnified and redeemed.

•

Today politicians claim to be building "a new world order" predicated on the "global economy." This particular version of "order" is destined to fail. Why? Because conventional economics is based on the principle of scarcity. And that which shrinks the many so the few can be enhanced ultimately implodes. It has throughout all history. The rise and fall of civilization after civilization has followed a similar path. The elevation comes when the remarkable energies of the masses are joined together to create synergistic possibilities previously only imaginable in the dream world. The fall comes in the wake of a select few accumulating far more than they need to thrive, with the masses being left with far less than they need to survive. What kind of a world order can hold itself together with just a few rich nations surrounded by hoards of poor ones?

In the economic structures human beings have constructed, money can be made only when there is scarcity. Back when water was freely available, it was not possible to make a dollar off it. However, once we poisoned the streams and showered the lakes with acid rain it became possible to sell bottled water. Today, there's no money in air, but if we pollute the atmosphere enough, some day there will be a fortune in bottled oxygen. In the economics of man (I suspect it's primarily a male mode of operating) either naturally or artificially created scarcity is necessary to make money.

What might be involved in creating economics based on the principles of abundance? I am not sure. However, I am

convinced that in my children's lifetime some noted econo-
mist, scientist, and theologian (I think it will require all three
disciplines coming together to achieve this) will win the Nobel
Prize for her paradigm-changing work titled *The Economics of
Abundance*.

Why am I so confident of this? Because I see people everywhere, in the corporate board rooms of America, in the black
villages of South Africa, in the lofty halls of Oxford University,
and in the resource-deprived schools of Mongolia yearning
for a new way. The current system does not satisfy the deep
longings of the heart anywhere. Even the truly wealthy, who
have achieved every advantage from this system, yearn for a
transformation in the realm of the spirit.

Today, everyone seems lost.

•

At MANNA we saw how collective lostness can spawn
liberation.

The manna that came to the wanderers in the wilderness
was so abundant and so miraculous that Moses taught his
people a special prayer:

> Blessed be Thou, O God our Lord, King of the world,
> who, in Thy bounty, dost provide for all the world;
> who in Thy grace, goodwill, and mercy,
> dost grant food to every creature,
> for Thy grace is everlasting.
> Thanks to Thy bounty we have never lacked for food,
> nor ever shall lack it, for Thy great name's sake.
> For Thou suppliest and providest for all;
> Thou art bountiful, and nourishest all Thy creatures
>   which Thou hast made.
> Blessed be Thou, O God, that dost provide for all.[24]

From MANNA I learned that

Every step we take is upon hallowed ground,
Every task we do is the Lord's work,
Every outstretched hand offered in love is the hand of
    God,
Every breath we take is spirit-filled,
Every moment we live is pregnant with transformative
    possibility.

NOTES

1. Donald Roth Kocher, *The Mother of Us All: First Presbyterian Church in Philadelphia, 1698–1998* (Woodbine, N.J.: Quinn Woodbine, 1998).

2. The students in my graduate class on "Group, Organizational, and Community Dynamics" who worked on the MANNA project were Penny Alexander, Natasha Bilimoria, Tina Bogart, Bonnie Cohen, Lance Daniels, David Eldridge, Michael Finucane, Catherine Fixe, Joshua Gold, Kaci Griffin, Eve Highstreet, Amy Hillier, Hoo-See (Karina) Kim, Rae Ann Knopf, Nicole Kubert, Patricia Loft, Judy Manin, Kevin Naskiewicz, Sara Roschwalb, David Rosenberg, Tasha Tervalon, Celeste Sanchez, Joe Surak, Sara (Vernon) Sterman, and Hui-Ching Wu.

3. This American Indian image was the basis of the poem "Lost" by David Wagoner, first published in David Whyte, *The House of Belonging* (Langley, Wash.: Many Rivers Press, 1997).

4. Published in the spring 1994 issue of *What's Cooking?* MANNA's quarterly newsletter.

5. Louis Ginsberg, *Legends of the Jews* (Philadelphia: Jewish Publication Society of America, 1911, 1939), 3:41.

6. Paul Tillich, *The Courage to Be* (New Haven: Yale University Press, 1952).

7. From Søren Kierkegaard, *Fear and Trembling*, as quoted by B. Friedman, *Writing Past Dark* (New York: Harper Perennial, 1993), 110, n. 8.

8. Friedman, *Writing Past Dark*, 110–11.

9. Ibid., 110.

10. Walter Brueggemann, "Loaves Abound," public lecture at Bryn Mawr Presbyterian Church, November 10, 2000.

11. Ginsberg, *Legends of the Jews*, 3:48.

12. See Dennis Linn, Sheila Fabricant Linn, and Matthew Linn, *Sleeping with Bread* (Mahwah N.J.: Paulist Press, 1995), 1.

13. Ginsberg, *Legends of the Jews*, 3:44.

14. The name of this fund-raiser and our partner, "UAS," referred to throughout this chapter have been fictionalized. The dynamics reported here, however, are exactly as we experienced them at the time.

15. Elizabeth Barret Browning, "Aurora Leigh," in *Aurora Leigh and Other Poems*, ed. John Robert Glorney Bolton and Julia Bolton Holloway (Harmondsworth, U.K.: Penguin, 1995), 821–22.

16. Published in the fall 1995 *What's Cooking*, MANNA's quarterly newsletter.

17. Brueggemann, "Loaves Abound."

18. Irving M. Bunim, *Ethics from the Sinai* (New York: Phillip Feldheim, 1964), 3:86–87.

19. A buddy serves as a caretaker for those living with AIDS who cannot look after themselves.

20. See Kenwyn K. Smith, *Groups in Conflict: Prisons in Disguise* (Dubuque, Ia.: Kendall-Hunt, 1982); and B. Oshry, *Leading Systems* (San Francisco: Berrett-Kohler, 1999).

21. The actual details have been changed to protect the identities of all parties, but the essence of this story is exactly as recounted here.

22. Again the date has been changed by a few weeks.

23. Walter Brueggemann, "How Much Is Left Over?" public lecture at Bryn Mawr Presbyterian Church, November 11, 2000.

24. Ginsberg, *Legends of the Jews*, 3:50.